Our True Beloved

Our True Beloved

Studies in Christianity and History Inspired
by *The Four Loves*

MICHAEL S. WHITING

WIPF & STOCK · Eugene, Oregon

OUR TRUE BELOVED
Studies in Christianity and History Inspired by *The Four Loves*

Copyright © 2024 Michael S. Whiting. All rights reserved. Except for brief quotations in critical publications or reviews, no part of this book may be reproduced in any manner without prior written permission from the publisher. Write: Permissions, Wipf and Stock Publishers, 199 W. 8th Ave., Suite 3, Eugene, OR 97401.

Wipf & Stock
An Imprint of Wipf and Stock Publishers
199 W. 8th Ave., Suite 3
Eugene, OR 97401

www.wipfandstock.com

PAPERBACK ISBN: 978-1-6667-3335-8
HARDCOVER ISBN: 978-1-6667-2792-0
EBOOK ISBN: 978-1-6667-2793-7

VERSION NUMBER 101024

All Scripture quotations, unless otherwise indicated, are taken from the Holy Bible, New International Version®, NIV®. Copyright ©1973, 1978, 1984, 2011 by Biblica, Inc.™ Used by permission of Zondervan. All rights reserved worldwide. www.zondervan.com. The "NIV" and "New International Version" are trademarks registered in the United States Patent and Trademark Office by Biblica, Inc.™

Scripture quotations marked (KJV) are taken from the KING JAMES VERSION, public domain.

Scripture quotations marked (NKJV) are taken from the New King James Version®. Copyright © 1982 by Thomas Nelson. Used by permission. All rights reserved.

Contents

Acknowledgments | vii
Introduction | ix
    The Four Loves in Ancient Literature (In Brief) | xv
    The Four Loves: A Framework | xvi

1 *Storge*: Loving God in the Habits of Christian Liturgy | 1
    Storge: The Habits of Liturgy and the Church as Mother | 2
    The Benefits and Limits of Liturgical *Storge* | 11

2 *Philia*: Loving God in Friendship with Christ | 19
    Philia: Friendship with Christ | 22
    The Age of Reason, Modern Philosophy, and the Moral Jesus | 39

3 *Eros*: Loving God in Desire for Personal Union | 47
    Eros: Desiring Spiritual Union with God | 49
    Spiritual *Eros*: Need and Excess | 64

4 *Agape*: Loving God "Unconditionally" through Pain | 75
    Agape: Loving God without Condition | 78
    Loving God with *Agape*: "Judge Not the Lord" | 85

5 Fractured Loves and the Secular Age | 87
    The Myth of Modern Progress and the New Humanity | 91
    The Same Old Story: Eden and Babel | 100
    Integration of the Four Loves and Christianity in a Secular Age | 103

Afterword: A Dialogue of the Four Loves | 106

Bibliography | 113

Acknowledgments

I want to thank Dr. Philip Mitchell, director of the honors program at Dallas Baptist University, for giving me an opportunity to tease out this idea between 2021 and 2023 on several occasions at Friday Symposiums and at the annual honors retreat.

I am grateful to my colleague and friend Dr. Mark Cook for our engaging daily conversations in philosophy, theology, and literature. I am inspired by your commitment to thoughtful education and your desire to push our students intellectually and spiritually even as you demonstrate a personal delight for learning.

As always, I am thankful for my wife, Julia, who is my best friend and companion—and at the time of writing has shared the journey of life with me for twenty-five years.

Thank you to the editorial team at Wipf and Stock who continue to be an outstanding and supportive partner in providing an avenue for me to express my fascination with the history of ideas.

The faults of this work are my own. I know this work will not answer all the questions it provokes, and it does not attempt to resolve all the problems of living Christianly in this modern world, but if it sheds light on the varieties of historical Christian movements and opens a conversation about what the Christian love of God still has to offer our twenty-first-century world, then I will consider it worth the while.

Michael S. Whiting
August 2, 2024

Introduction

HISTORICAL CHRISTIANITY IS A "mosaic."[1] It is Christianity as it developed across thousands of years of history, in changing cultural landscapes and political contexts, that gave us new expressions and forms in Roman Catholicism, Eastern Orthodoxy, Anglicanism, Methodism, Baptists, Presbyterianism, Messianic Judaism, Churches of Christ, Assemblies of God, Bible churches, and the list goes on. If there is anything that can be said of Christianity in the twenty-first century, it's that it is diverse—and bewilderingly so.

On the one hand, this fragmentation and division can be viewed tragically, which many did in the aftermath of the sixteenth- and seventeenth-century European wars of religion. Fighting for territory, in defense of religious conscience, or for control of government between Protestants and Catholics took the lives of millions in its wake. If there ever was a time to ask what had become of Christ's prayer in John 17 for his church to be one, it was then. Voltaire, a French Enlightenment philosopher in the eighteenth century, expressed a vigorous disaffection for organized, established Christianity among European states and the social ruptures caused by division, which arguably gave birth to philosophies of confessional disestablishment promoted by modern deists and atheists, as well as nonconformist Christian communities.[2]

On the other hand, Christianity's resistance in history against *uniformity* has allowed it to flourish enduringly, especially where this was a viable political option, as observed by the nineteenth-century French spectator of American democracy Alexis de Tocqueville.[3] Where a degree of Christian

---

1. Olson, *Mosaic of Christian Belief*.
2. Larsen, *Friends of Religious Equality*.
3. Tocqueville, *Democracy in America*, 478–88.

Introduction

pluralism is appreciated, each movement can be seen as offering a unique challenge and contribution to the whole church. This was the perspective of Count Nicholas Zinzendorf, the eighteenth-century German Pietist, leader of the Moravian Brethren (*Unitas Fratrum*), and a pioneer of Christian ecumenism.[4] Each new movement emerged to correct (and often overcorrected) what neglect or excess had distorted in the ever-swinging, reactionary pendulum of history. As church historian Euan Cameron states, "Christian history is, in large part, the history of shifting emphases, of a constant tendency to stress one feature of the Christian message over another, and to veer to extremes of some sort or other."[5] Historians of global Christianity and contemporary missiologists also point to the faith's freedom to culturally, linguistically, and theologically diversify as one explanatory cause for its flourishing in the Majority World, especially over the last one hundred years, with more confessing believers in Jesus across the earth than ever before.[6]

Christianity, however we may want to define its core doctrines, was and always is incarnated in the historical process, and thus its developing expression through the centuries bears an inescapable relationship to human creatureliness (and with respect to human frailty, sin). To associate one tradition or denomination as possessing the whole corner of the truth as *the* Christianity (my own evangelical Baptist background included) underestimates the limitations and imperfections of human beings who see "through a glass darkly" (1 Cor 13:12 KJV)[7] and binds the freedom of the Spirit of God who blows where he pleases (John 3:8).

Each historical tradition offers something to appreciate as well as to criticize as incomplete, and Christians across many traditions have been known to think and act in ways that were blatantly unworthy of any association with Jesus' name at all. As Lewis stated,

> If ever the book which I am not going to write is written it must be the full confession by Christendom of Christendom's contribution to the sum of human cruelty and treachery. Large areas of "the World" will not hear us till we have publicly disowned much of our

---

4. Each denomination possesses a "jewel of truth . . . particular to itself." Lewis, *Zinzendorf*, 101–11.

5. Cameron, *Interpreting Christian History*, 103.

6. Walls, *Missionary Movement*, 3–15; McGrath, *Christianity's Dangerous Idea*.

7. There were probably few churches in the apostolic period as divided as Corinth.

Introduction

past. Why should they? We have shouted the name of Christ and enacted the service of Moloch.[8]

With this acknowledgment, I am not defining Christianity as a vague spiritual or moral essence without any historical or dogmatic basis. Rather, to borrow Lewis's aphorism of "mere Christianity,"[9] when I refer to Christianity in this book, I am speaking broadly for what George Calixtus, amid the sixteenth-century rending of the church in theological divisions, appealed to as the "consensus of the first five centuries."[10] This might be too generous of a definition of Christianity for some readers, including those of my own evangelical Protestant heritage in the Baptist tradition, but the complexities of history and human fallibility across two thousand years around the world has discouraged me from being too rash in equating Christianity with, and asserting a spiritual superiority of, one branch of Christians. Although it may be more complicated and probably feels less safe, I believe it is wisest to approach history with humility, to listen and understand first, before making judgments. As Lewis himself says in *The Four Loves*, "The human mind is generally far more eager to praise and dispraise than to describe and define."[11]

Other astute readers might rightly critique the focus in my book largely, though not exclusively, on Christianity's occidental trajectory, and—beginning with the sixteenth century—on Protestant history. Given the purpose of the book, which is not intended to provide a comprehensive historical look at Christianity but to identify some examples from movements of Catholic, Orthodox, Protestant, and Pentecostal/Charismatic traditions, I hope this will be forgiven.[12]

The peculiar idea behind this book is the fruit of my own personal fascination for C. S. Lewis's sadly more underrated masterpiece, *The Four Loves*. I am not a Lewis expert, but neither is this book intended to primarily

---

8. Lewis, *Four Loves*, 30. To ignore the darker side of Christian history would be like removing a substantial proportion of the history of Israel from the Scriptures. See 1 Cor 10:11.

9. Lewis, *Mere Christianity*, in *Signature Classics*, 1–178.

10. Viz., the christological and Trinitarian doctrines established at Nicaea (325), Constantinople (381), Ephesus (435), and Chalcedon (451). Callisen, "Georg Calixtus," 1–23.

11. Lewis, *Four Loves*, 12.

12. I hope that readers will view the wider richness of historical Christian thought as a treasure available to the whole church.

Introduction

be about Lewis or even *The Four Loves*.[13] I have returned to Lewis's insightful Christian perspective on love many times in recent years. The dynamics that he explores bring to light this core, multifaceted, and mysterious quality of our personal identity and social existence as God's crowning creatures. To love reflects the reality that our self-conscious personhood needs communion and reciprocal love with other persons to experience the fullness of human flourishing. For Christians who believe in God as Trinity, this makes logical sense. For before anything else was created, there was God, and this God was an eternal relationship of Father, Son, and Holy Spirit existing in the perfection of reciprocal love. The church father Augustine even used the human analogy of love to illustrate the Trinity: "But when we came to charity, which is called God in holy scripture, the glimmerings of a trinity began to appear, namely lover and what is loved and love."[14] When God determined to create this material world, and especially to create mankind to be the paramount visible image of himself, would it not be expected that they would reflect their maker God as one and many, both unity and personal plurality? In fact, one might argue that the whole tragic story of humanity can be summed up as the fracturing of love in God's originally perfect "uni-verse." A whole book has yet to be written that looks into the philosophical, economic, religious, and political movements of history from the perspective of this tension and the shifting polarity between the one and the many—humanity's ultimate inability to resolve a balance between individual personality and the common good.[15] In Christian theology, this broken trinitarian image of love is only finally healed and overcome by God, in *the self-giving love of the Many as One*—the love the Son shows for the Father, and the Father for the Son, and the Holy Spirit for the Father and Son. The church, especially, is called to live in the Spirit as a model of the Trinity in reconciling the many as one in love and community (John 17:20–26).[16]

---

13. Thus, my choice of the subtitle "Inspired by."

14. Augustine, *Trinity*, 514. On the Trinity as "society" in Lewis, see *The Problem of Pain*, in *Signature Classics*, 562; Peterson, *C. S. Lewis*, 104–8.

15. Although Lewis does not tie this to the doctrine of the Trinity directly, he also sees the twin polar dangers of Individualism (separation from the single "organism" of humanity) and Totalitarianism (suppression of individual organs within one organism). See Lewis, *Mere Christianity*, in *Signature Classics*, 150. On the difference between human individuals who exist for the city and the eternal destiny of human persons for whom the city exists, see Maritain, *Three Reformers*, 16–18.

16. See Volf, *After Our Likeness*, especially Part 2.

Introduction

For the last twenty years, I have been pondering this problem of the one and many in historical Christianity. Movements and shifts developed that offered critique and correction but appeared often to lose something in the process of reaction, which perhaps was not as clear or uncovered until later (which seemed to occur again and again). In reading *The Four Loves*, it occurred to me that perhaps what Lewis describes about human loves might also be true about *loving God*. Namely, could I see a correspondence between Lewis's distinguishing between four loves—*storge, philia, eros,* and *agape*—and four emphases and expressions of loving God in various movements and traditions within historical Christianity? Furthermore, as Lewis discusses the blessings and distortions of each love in the context of human relationships (except *agape*), perhaps there are ways Christians have loved God in history that are complementary but were, in fact, fragmented and conflicted due to excesses. That is the ambitious aim of this book.

This is not a comprehensive study of the *The Four Loves* in all its layers, facets, and issues, including some rather chauvinist comments about women that will certainly not hold up today, so I strongly encourage readers to sit with the whole book on its own merit. Although Lewis's other writings will be mined to reinforce, develop, or support a point, it is not my intention to provide an exhaustive synthesis of the four loves and related themes across the entire corpus of Lewis's literary legacy. My initial purpose will be to identify and explain the essence of each love as Lewis defines them, including both their virtues and their vices, and with a specific eye toward using this framework as inspiration for interpreting movements within historical Christianity—Catholic, Orthodox, Protestant, and Pentecostal-Charismatic.[17]

The design of the book's argument, then, is admittedly not strictly historical. Its methodology uses an idea grid to interpret history and reflect on a particular theme—loving God. It engages Christian movements

---

17. For those familiar with Richard Foster's work, my approach may appear reminiscent of his book *Streams of Living Water*. Foster identifies six traditions or streams in Christian history: contemplative, holiness, charismatic, social justice, evangelical, and incarnational. He rightly sees in Jesus the perfect and holistic synthesis of all these traditions that often become more fractured in Christianity's history. The current study is not intended to compete with or replace Foster's insightful book but to offer another distinctive way to reflect critically on the mosaic of Christianity's broad history, uniquely using the lens of *The Four Loves*. Also, I believe there is some value in limiting the number of emphases so as not to overstate their distinguishable character. However, I do not intend to suggest that loving God is limited to these four modes. This book does not deal with sexual morality, global missions and evangelism, or vocational stewardship.

broadly across a very diverse range of social, cultural, and historical contexts, observing patterns and types through the critical lens of *The Four Loves*, which (a) engages ecumenically with the benefits and problems in various traditions and movements of historical Christianity, (b) suggests how the fracturing distortion of these loves in history may have partly contributed to the emergence of the modern humanist option, and (c) reflects on how their holistic and centered integration can offer a robust resistance to the pressures of secularism. As Niebuhr acknowledges in *Christ and Culture*, typology is an imperfect way of engaging and analyzing history. Distinguishing emphases and forms of love in the history of Christianity that often conflict or compete is not meant to suggest that these types are never integrated in individuals or movements. There are always dangers of oversimplification and anachronism. However, "although historically inadequate, [typology] has the advantage of calling to attention the continuity and significance of the great *motifs* that appear and reappear in the long wrestling of Christians with their enduring problem."[18] The enduring problem in this book is the oscillating weight given to different ways of loving God in the church's past and present.

I can sense that advanced students and scholars of Lewis also know full well that my plan and purpose take us beyond his own intentions in writing *The Four Loves*. Lewis's analysis—except perhaps *agape*—is focused on the loves *between humans*, how they become distorted by sin and are sanctified by grace in the *agape* of God. Yes, in Augustinian and Platonic fashion, Lewis describes how human loves are shadows of a higher love of God, in which all human loves become perfected. Indeed, natural human loves can "become rivals to spiritual loves: but they can also be preparatory imitations of it, training (so to speak) of the spiritual muscles which Grace may later put to a higher service."[19] However, Lewis does not delve into the analogical correspondence of each of the natural human loves to Christians' *love of God*. In fact, when discussing friendship love (*philia*), Lewis mentions in passing that this is mostly avoided by biblical writers as an analogy, unlike marriage or fatherhood, because viewing human friendship as a symbolic "nearness of likeness" (or "resemblance") could be misconstrued as an actual "nearness of approach."[20] Whether or not Lewis could or would affirm what I attempt to do in the pages that follow is debatable.

18. Niebuhr, *Christ and Culture*, 43–44.
19. Lewis, *Four Loves*, 24.
20. Lewis, *Four Loves*, 4–5, 87–88.

Introduction

The Four Loves in Ancient Literature (in Brief)

Lewis expressed his desire to craft an original Christian reflection on four Greek loves in a letter dated to 1958, describing the loves as "nearly the whole of Christian ethics."[21] Originally a series of radio broadcasts, *The Four Loves*, published in 1960, is a Christian synthesis of classical pagan and biblical philology. Apart from *agape* (what Lewis translates as "charity" from the Latin *caritas*), *eros*, *philia*, and *storge* were already in common use before New Testament times.[22] In Greek mythology, *eros* was personified as a god, the son of Aphrodite, and most often associated with sexual desire. The philosopher Plato in his *Symposium* stresses *eros* as the desire- or will-to-possess, but he equates this not with a desire for sexual union with a human being but rational union with the supreme idea of ultimate beauty.[23] Plato's student Aristotle, in three books of his *Nichomachean Ethics*, expounds on the primary human love of friendship (*philia*).

In the New Testament, by contrast, *eros* is nowhere present (and rarely found in the Greek Septuagint), but variations of *storge*, *philia*, and *agape* appear. The word used instead of *eros* in the Gospels and Epistles is *epithumeo* and is always negative in connotation in sins of sexual passion. *Storge* is found in 2 Tim 3:4 as *astorgous* ("without affection," KJV) and in Rom 12:10 as *philostorgoi* ("affectioned," KJV). *Philia* is the second most common New Testament Greek word translated as love. It appears over fifty times (n. *philos*, v. *phileo*), including such passages as Matt 6:5, John 16:27, 1 Cor 16:22, Titus 3:15, and Rev 3:19. The most common rendering of love in the New Testament is *agape*, which occurs over three hundred times (*agapao*, *agapetos*), such as in John 15:9, Rom 13:10, Eph 2:4, and 1 Pet 4:8. *Agape* and *philia* are used interchangeably when connoting the affection between friends, family, disciples, and the goodwill of God toward mankind. *Philia*, however, is never used of human love for God, and *agape* extends uniquely to a love for enemies.[24]

---

21. Lewis to Bishop Henry Louttit, Jan. 5, 1958, in *Collected Letters*, 3:941. See also "Letter to a Priest," in *Collected Letters*, 3:1035–36.

22. Lewis to Warnie, May 4, 1940, in *Collected Letters*, 2:408.

23. Plato, *Symposium*, in Cohen, et al., *Readings*, 260–61; Nygren, *Agape and Eros*, 175–77.

24. Bromiley, *International Standard Bible Encyclopedia*, 3:175; Hahn, *Catholic Bible Dictionary*, 553.

Introduction

The Four Loves: A Framework

In the opening chapters of *The Four Loves*, Lewis makes an initial and foundational distinction between "Need-love" and "Gift-love," which are "mutually illuminating" to his whole discussion of the corruptions and sanctification of the four loves.[25] Lewis discovered in contemplating the nature of love that Need-loves simply make us human creatures: "We are born helpless."[26] We depend upon others (a child upon a mother), and we experience "Need-pleasure" in satisfying our most basic human needs (water for thirst or food for hunger). Yet Need-loves can fall into moral danger. For example, the love of *storge*, between parents and children, is part of human nurturing, but "a tyrannous and gluttonous demand for affection can be a horrible thing."[27] Even Gift-love can become an evil to the degree we "give our human loves the unconditional allegiance we owe only to God."[28] Anders Nygren contrasted too simplistically the divine selflessness of *agape* and the human selfishness of *eros*.[29] There is evil in all human loves for Lewis, and it is more about whether a Need-love becomes excessive demand or Gift-love becomes a form of subconscious manipulative control. Any human love that robs God of his preeminent throne in the human heart is rendered corruptible: "The rivalry between all natural loves and the love of God is something a Christian dare not forget. God is the great Rival."[30] Our most important love is his love for us and our love for him, "our true Beloved."[31]

Need-loves and Need-pleasures are to be distinguished from "Appreciation-pleasures," like admiring a beautiful sunset on the edge of an ocean view. We do not need them to live, says Lewis. They are "super-added" gifts. However, through an addiction for pleasure, they can also morph into something harmful, from Appreciation-pleasures to *Need*-pleasures.[32]

---

25. Caroline J. Simon, "On Love," in MacSwain and Ward, *Cambridge Companion*, 147–49.

26. Lewis, *Four Loves*, 2.

27. Lewis, *Four Loves*, 2–3.

28. Lewis, *Four Loves*, 8.

29. Lewis to Janet Spens, Jan. 8, 1935, in *Collected Letters*, 2:153; Lewis to Mary Van Deusen, Dec. 4, 1954, in *Collected Letters*, 3:538; Lepojärvi, "Praeparatio Evangelica," 208–9.

30. Lewis, *Four Loves*, 38.

31. Lewis, *Four Loves*, 140.

32. Lewis, *Four Loves*, 10–12.

INTRODUCTION

Before God, all human creatures approach him in Need-love. Our very life and breath come from him. In view of our sin, we stand in even greater need of his mercy to provide a way of salvation. Although Lewis acknowledges a love of God purely for himself,[33] what he refers to as a pure "Gift" or "Appreciation love,"[34] he also knows that no creature approaches God in this life entirely or purely free of all self-interest.[35] Although we may experience our greatest "nearness-of-approach" to God in our Gift-love toward others,[36] only God exists above Need-love. In fact, this is a chief attribute of his that sets him apart. He is wholly self-sufficient and only ever Gift-love. He needed nothing before creation and even after creation remains pure Gift-love, according to Lewis. Elsewhere, he states that "God has no needs," and that if it can be said that God desires our relationship, this was self-imposed by his own will and for our good: "If he who himself can lack nothing chooses to need us, it is because we need to be needed."[37]

Following this discussion, Lewis then introduces the critical idea that he weaves throughout *The Four Loves*, which is that each kind of love "begins to be a demon only when he begins to be a god." Like Augustine, but perhaps with less contempt toward human loves,[38] Lewis emphasizes that all human loves must be ordered underneath the love of God: "The created glory may be expected to give us hints of the uncreated; for the one is derived from the other and some fashion reflects it."[39] Yet, given the essential human quality and power of love, if divorced from loving God first, it then becomes an evil, and the love of anything created thereby becomes harmful as it is loosed: "For natural loves that are allowed to become gods do not remain loves. They are still called so but can become in fact complicated

---

33. Bernard, "On Loving God," in *Selected Works*, 175–76, 194. Lewis was an admirer of Bernard as he was of other mystical writers. See Downing, *Region of Awe*, 71.

34. Lewis, *Four Loves*, 17.

35. Lewis, *Four Loves*, 4; Lepojärvi, "Praeparatio Evangelica," 208–9.

36. Lewis, *Four Loves*, 5–6.

37. Lewis, *Four Loves*, 2, 4, 126–29; Lewis, *Problem of Pain*, in *Signature Classics*, 576.

38. Although Lewis shares with Plato and Augustine an emphasis on earthly pleasures as shadows or images of a superior, eternal beauty, he is less disparaging of the pleasures of the senses. Tiffany, "Anti-Platonic Platonist," 357–58; Hansen, "Friendship," 19–30; Peterson, *C. S. Lewis*, 9–12.

39. Lewis, *Four Loves*, 21. See also Lewis, *Letters to Malcolm*, 89–90. "We remain conscious of a desire that no natural happiness will satisfy." Lewis, "Weight of Glory," in *Weight of Glory*, 3–6.

forms of hatred."[40] To say "all we need is love" is a vague and naïve notion when one reflects on the dark potentialities of twisted human love when separated from divine love himself.[41] Natural human loves, given an inordinate, deified position separate from divine love himself, become evils and powerfully destructive, much like the Opera Phantom's deadly Need-love for his musical pupil Christine Daaé or in the erotic Need-love for Count Vronsky that led to the adultery, paranoia, and tragic suicide of Tolstoy's Anna Karenina. Even a Gift-love in self-sacrificing, patriotic affection for a nation can become harmful when it uncritically participates in imperialistic ambitions or injustice against innocents.[42] Familial affection can breed possessiveness, jealousy, and resentment. In the biblical story of Jacob and Esau, it split a family through favoritism and deception (Gen 27). Love that favors one (or some) is naturally and unavoidably love withheld from others, and the result is pain.

The remaining outline of Lewis's book explores the unique delight and depravity of each of the three human loves—*storge, philia, eros*—and concludes with the perfection of divine love in *agape*. Chapters 2 through 5 of this book will develop these loves in greater detail, but a summary here will suffice. *Storge* (affection) is defined by Lewis as the love developed through familiarity and a sense of belonging more quietly nurtured through the sharing of time and proximity, especially within the family unit. In the chapter on *storge*, I attempt to bridge a connection with the church as family and the love of God nurtured in historical Christian liturgy and spiritual habits centered on word and sacrament. Integrating some of the recent work done by James Smith and other historians of Christian liturgy, the emphasis on loving God here is that formed and expressed through the language, the stories, the beliefs, and the symbols that shape the Christian love of God through familiarity and repetition, even in unconscious ways.

Philia (friendship) love is essentially the sharing of a common vision of reality or valuing the same truth, which Lewis himself experienced at Oxford with fellow writers Charles Williams, J. R. R. Tolkien, and others of the Inklings.[43] In my chapter on *philia*, the emphasis here falls on ways in which Christians in history have acted in union with the mind and heart of

---

40. Lewis, *Four Loves*, 6, 8, 28.

41. Vainio, "Aporia of Arguments," 21–30.

42. Lewis warns of the dangers of an uncritical patriotism and love of country in *Four Loves*, 22–30.

43. Glyer, *Bandersnatch*.

INTRODUCTION

Jesus and the realities of his kingdom, loving God through the sacrifice of obedience in ministries of mercy, compassion, and justice. Although Lewis argued that *philia* as a human love is a poor analogy to compare with love for God, I suggest that Jesus' own words to his disciples—that to be his "friends" is to do his will, which is also that of the Father (John 15:14–16)—can be applied.[44]

Eros (desire) is a desire for union between the sexes. It is inclusive of, but not limited to, sexual union. In this chapter, I will trace movements in historical Christianity that have expressed the love of God as a longing for an experience of intimate union with God that touches the soul through practices of withdrawal and solitude, the disciplines of contemplation, prayer, and meditation on Scripture, as well as individual experience in communal worship. Stress will be laid on the effects of *eros* in heightened spiritual emotions of love, joy, and peace and even manifestations of God's power in charismatic gifts.

Finally, Lewis concludes his book with *agape* (charity), the unconditional, selfless love perfected in the extreme generosity of God toward sinful creatures. This love gives without expectation or need. It can sanctify the other loves corrupted by selfishness, but it also extends beyond familial bonds, circles of friendship, and joys of marital union to the most unworthy enemies devoid of anything to otherwise attract our love. Charity is set apart by Lewis from the other loves as an act of pure disinterested choice and will, of deontological duty. "So you also, when you have done everything you were told to do, should say, 'We are unworthy servants; we have only done our duty'" (Luke 17:10). How does one apply charity (*agape*), or divine Gift-love, toward God himself who *is* worthy? To love God unconditionally without self-interest, what Lewis calls "supernatural Appreciative love," is difficult, if not impossible, to achieve or sustain as sinners, let alone as creatures. The focus of this chapter is on loving God in obedience through suffering, especially unexplained afflictions—to love God who might at times *feel* difficult to love.

Lewis believed that without limits and boundaries the human loves of *storge*, *philia*, and *eros* become destructive. The power and high nobility of each love is humbled by the reality of their potential corruption in excess when unmoored from God. If we allow them to become gods, they will thereby become demons. My argument is that the same can be said of the

---

44. See also Jas 4:4–8 that contrasts friendship with the world system as enmity with God.

Introduction

various emphases of loving God in historical Christianity. When one love of God was allowed to become prominent to the exclusion or diminishing of the others, even excessive *agape*, such extremes harmed the full testimony of the Christian life and provoked movements of reaction—some which moved beyond the pale of orthodoxy.

It is important to acknowledge the scores of Christians in history in whom the four loves were integrated holistically, where the contemplative life (*eros*) merged with the active life (*philia*) and the practice of communal liturgical worship (*storge*) with the endurance of afflictions (*agape*). Yet, oftentimes, even where overemphasis, neglect, or a conflict was *perceived*, reaction *did* in fact lead to excess and an actual severing of the loves to harmful consequences, including movements of mystical individualism that negated the value of liturgical worship in organized churches, as well as modern secular ethics born from the Enlightenment that divorced moral action—even when holding up Jesus as an exemplar—from the supernatural empowerment of the prayerful, contemplative life and the habits of liturgical Christian worship. Orthodox scholar Alexander Schmemann refers to such a historical clash between those Christians who have emphasized private contemplation and an other-worldly kingdom ("spiritualists") and Christians who have primarily busied themselves in bettering the kingdom of *this* present world ("activists"): "We are constantly called to repent for having spent too much time in contemplation and adoration, silence and liturgy, for not having dealt sufficiently with the social, political, economic, racial, and all other issues of real life."[45] This statement sounds remarkably like words spoken by Elder Zosima, a Russian Orthodox monk, in Dostoyevsky's *Brothers Karamazov*.[46] It was also a question considered by ancient Greek philosophers, Plato as well as Aristotle, who both concluded that the contemplative life is superior to even the rational ordering of the historical.[47]

---

45. Schmemann, *Life of the World*, 18–19. On the tension between the contemplative and the active life, see also Okholm, *Monk Habits*, 29; Leiva-Merikakis, *Love's Sacred Order*, 18–19; Armstrong, *Medieval Wisdom*, 227–28.

46. "Obedience, fasting and prayer are even the objects of laughter.... The monk is reproached for his solitariness: 'You have withdrawn into solitariness to save yourself, living the life of a monk within monastery walls, and have forgotten the brotherly service of mankind.' But we shall see which of them will be more diligent in the matter of brotherly love. For the solitariness is not ours, but theirs, only they do not see it." Dostoyevsky, *Brothers Karamazov*, 407.

47. Niebuhr, *Faith and History*, 61–62.

INTRODUCTION

My hope is that Lewis's *The Four Loves* will help us to interpret this pendulum in Christianity's historical development and perhaps illuminate the challenge and necessity of holding these in a better tension. Looking at multiple traditions of historical Christianity, rather than allowing these loves to drift into extremes that diminish the faith once for all delivered, a more integrated balance will sustain a holistic Christianity—a vibrant faith that pushes back, rather than reinforces, the cultural current of modern secular humanism that a diminished Christianity even helped to produce.

1

Storge

Loving God in the Habits of Christian Liturgy

"I BEGIN WITH THE humblest and most widely diffused of loves, the love in which our experience seems to differ least from that of the animals."[1] So Lewis begins his analysis of *storge*, which he defines primarily as familial "affection," but he also extends this love beyond to classmates, shipmates, animals, or really any person, group, or thing toward which we have developed a slow, growing, and oftentimes subconscious attachment through the sharing of time and a certain proximity. Less like the more palpable love of romance or collaborative vision of friendship, to become aware of affection "is to become aware that it has already been going on for some time." In fact, it is often not until the object is lost that the strength of affection comes to the surface: "Affection almost slinks or seeps through our lives."[2] The objects of *storge* are often most easily taken for granted. Yet, *storge* is also "responsible for nine-tenths of whatever solid and durable happiness there is in our natural lives."[3]

Among the four loves, *storge* has the least to do with choice. Whether "put down by fate in the same household or community," affection arises toward "the people who happen to be there." Of all the loves, it is the "most catholic" and the least discriminating in the sense that it has little or nothing

---

1. Lewis, *Four Loves*, 31.
2. Lewis, *Four Loves*, 33–34.
3. Lewis, *Four Loves*, 53.

to do with a sharing of age, gender, social class, educational level, or even species. "Almost anyone may be the object of affection," and one perversion therein Lewis identifies is that "almost everyone expects" to receive it. The "ease and informality" with which *storge* grows in our familiarity and security of acceptance can negate the intentionality that makes us worthy of it. As the adage states, "familiarity can breed contempt," and "old" can be a term of endearment as well as reproach.[4]

One perversion of *storge* is when Gift-love becomes a Need-love, in the sense that the Giver's whole identity is bound up in the pride of being indispensable to the receiver, forming unhealthy attachments of codependency. This was the experience of Catherine toward her fatherless family in Ward's novel *Robert Elsmere*: "An egregious over-estimate of her own value. . . . And religious scruple, for her torment, showed her her past, transformed, alloyed with all sorts of personal prides and cravings, which stood unmasked now in a white light."[5]

Relatedly, a perversion of *storge* as a Need-love is in its jealousy, like the mother Pam in Lewis's *Great Divorce* who loved her son to the excess of wanting him to leave heaven to join her in hell: "Pam, Pam—no natural feelings are high or low, holy or unholy, in themselves. They are all holy when God's hand is on the rein. They all go bad when they set up their own and make themselves into false gods."[6] Any change can be "a threat to Affection," and change is viewed as loss—"its reliance on what is old and familiar." Affection can also be taken for granted or slighted by the object of *storge*, which can poison the lover's heart with bitter resentment, and like the other loves, "carry . . . the seeds of hatred."[7]

Storge: The Habits of Liturgy and the Church as Mother

As *storge* (affection) is nurtured through familiarity and the sharing of time and space, it could also be said that our love and affection for God can similarly be developed, formed, nurtured, and expressed through the culture of belonging and the familiar structures of organized, communal habits of worship (liturgy). The least conscious and deliberative form of love, building an affection towards God over time through the structured patterns and

---

4. Lewis, *Four Loves*, 40–43.
5. Ward, *Robert Elsmere*, 161.
6. Lewis, *Great Divorce*, in *Signature Classics*, 518–20.
7. Lewis, *Four Loves*, 45, 55–56.

habits of worship may grow more unnoticed or may seem to be in danger of indifference through repetition, yet on that same account *storge* can also be the most durable and rooted love compared with the others.

Since the dawning of Christianity within its first-century Jewish context, Christians have gathered for worship and spiritual nurture and formation in communities, sometimes from birth. The church is the communal context in which Christians are formed (and re-formed) in spirit, mind, and body, orienting them toward the love of God as his fallen and yet redeemed-by-love people. Gathering to participate collectively in the habits of prayer, musical praise, submission to the word, and sharing in the sacraments of baptism and communion as a spiritual family not only binds Christians to one another in relationship with God, but the simple act of gathering is a public, corporate recognition of thanksgiving and dependence upon him for all temporal and eternal gifts.

The word denoting the organized structure of a worship service, "liturgy" (from the Greek *leitourgia*, which means "work of the people") is technically misleading. Christians gather to offer their worship and obedience in "thanksgiving" (in Greek *eucharistia*) *because* of the prior work of God in Jesus who continues to extend the summons and invitation to come to him as individuals and in community to be spiritually restored by his presence always at work. Each week, Christians gather at the invitation and calling of God who himself opened the way through Jesus to his glory, renewing individually and collectively their commitment to see themselves and the world through the truth of God's self-revelation. To join in Christian worship is to embody a counter-story and meaning to life that challenges not only rival metaphysical philosophies and religions, but the independent and proud humanism of modern deism and atheism. This weekly gathering of Christians (a ritual) is not separate from but continuous with the whole service (liturgy) of daily human life before God, offering the creation he made back to him as a priestly sacrifice of praise (Rom 12:1–2).[8]

With the exception perhaps of seventeenth-century Friends (or Quaker) meetings, the weekly assembling of Christians has historically followed some form of prepared order. It may be simpler or more complex, but there are standard elements shared by every Sunday gathering (or Saturday in the case of Messianic Jews or Seventh-day Adventists), which can be traced back to Christianity's Jewish synagogue origins.

---

8. Schmemann, *Life of the World*, 44–58.

Ancient Traditions

While the New Testament church may appear more decentralized and dynamic in its primitive stages, the Pauline epistles demonstrate that before the end of the first century, and in response to various pastoral issues, there were instructions put in place to improve public order and unity among the growing network of churches.[9] That order continued to develop in the three centuries that followed as Christianity sprawled throughout the Roman world, baptizing more people from pagan backgrounds and hedging the apostolic faith against the rise of heresies such as Gnosticism. Documents dating to the second to third centuries, including Justin Martyr's *First Apology*, the *Didache (Teaching of the Twelve Apostles)*, and *The Apostolic Tradition*, reveal a diverse, but increasingly organized formula, especially for administrating the ceremonial rite of initiation in baptism and the communal celebration of the Lord's Supper under an ordained hierarchy of bishops and priests.[10] Then, with the changing relationship of church and state following the conversion of Emperor Constantine and the Roman Empire in the fourth to fifth centuries, the forms of Christian worship—including the funding and construction of grandiose public buildings—moved toward even more elaborate ritual and uniform structures.[11] A high degree of ceremonial ritual in fourth-century Christian worship naturally developed in the context of a culture that revered imperial and monarchial authority. As Jesus was seen as the supreme sovereign of the universe, and as the earthly worship service was meant to join through earthly mediation and imitation in the heavenly court of praise, it was natural that ancient Roman (and later medieval) Christians would approach the mystery of worship on earth as entrance into a cosmic royal ceremony in heaven. This form understandably continued in the churches of the medieval, Renaissance, and early Protestant Reformation eras until becoming challenged by the increasing separation of the spiritual from the symbolic, along with declining belief in divine-right monarchies in favor of more republican and democratic forms of religious and political government.

---

9. For example, see 1 Cor 14.

10. Justin Martyr, "First Apology," 285–87; Milavec, *Didache*; Hippolytus, *On the Apostolic Tradition*.

11. For an overview of the ancient liturgical developments, see Ross and Lamport, *Historical Foundations*; González and González, *Worship in the Early Church*; Wainwright and Westerfield Tucker, *Oxford History*; White, *Brief History*.

Nevertheless, a common tradition of weekly attendance to "Word and Table" remained the basic pattern for most Christians as set forth early on by Justin Martyr in his *First Apology* of the second century:[12]

> And on the day called Sunday there is a meeting in one place of those who live in the cities or the country, and the memoirs of the apostles or the writings of the prophets are read as long as time permits. When the reader has finished, the president in a discourse urges and invites to the admonition of these noble things. Then we all stand together and offer prayers. And, as said before, when we have finished the prayer, bread is brought, and wine and water, and the president similarly sends up prayers and thanksgivings to the best of his ability, and the congregation assents, saying the Amen; the distribution, and reception of the consecrated [elements] by each one, takes place and they are sent to the absent by the deacons.[13]

Latin Roman Catholicism, Orthodox churches of the Greek, Syrian, and Russian East, as well as the older Protestant traditions of Europe and Britain—Anglicans (and Methodists), Lutherans, and Presbyterians—created diverse church orders from a common liturgical heritage that displayed the sharing of these fundamental elements:[14]

- singing of psalms and hymns
- responsory prayers (e.g., confession)
- several readings from Scripture (Old Testament, Gospels, Epistles)
- recitation of ancient creeds
- weekly participation in the Eucharist (Lord's Supper or Communion)

Christians since at least the fourth century also experienced the yearly cycle of time in liturgical celebration of key moments in redemptive history centered on Jesus: Annunciation of Christ's birth in March through the four Sundays of Advent and Christmas in December; Epiphany after the start of the New Year; Palm Sunday through the Easter Season in March or April; Ascension Day and Pentecost forty to fifty days after Easter. Whereas people today tell the time of year more by the changing of seasons or professional sports schedules, Christians relearned all the major events in the

---

12. Phillips, "Worship in the Early Church," 51–52.
13. Justin Martyr, "First Apology," 287; Chan, *Liturgical Theology*, 68–69.
14. We might call this "Mere Christianity" in its *liturgical* form.

life and ministry of Christ from his conception to his present heavenly intercession, and each yearly cycle retold the coming of Jesus in a way that made him the focus of every year and the turning point of all history until its completion: "Observing the seasons of the church year also helps us embrace the church's telling of time instead of our culture's. . . . Rooted in time, in community and in the greatest, truest story of all, the church year focuses our attention, moment by moment, season by season, year after year, on the one thing that is needful, enabling us to enter together into the very life of God as he enters into life with us."[15]

Along with the liturgy of Sunday worship and the special services of the church calendar, a practice of daily hours of prayer developed among churches of the first three centuries. Common among them was a threefold daily prayer, often in the morning, noon, and evening, after the pattern of the Old Testament prophet Daniel or in connection with the hours of Christ's sufferings on the cross. These prayers were practiced in private and in smaller gatherings of families, but often in this early period, believers gathered all together for daily hours of prayer.[16] This latter practice survived in the monasteries, which for Benedictines included seven separate hours of dedicated prayer throughout the day and evening (Ps 119:64), and once in the middle of the night (Ps 119:62, 147), balanced in proportion with their tasks of manual labor to support the community.[17]

Protestant and Evangelical Liturgies

Out of the Protestant Reformation, in a desire to reform the corruptions of late medieval Catholicism by returning to the simpler descriptions of Christian worship in the New Testament more closely, worship services of many Protestant traditions became to various degrees decreasingly structured and complex in ritual.

Most Protestant churches of the sixteenth century followed a modified, and much reduced, annual church calendar of special days of

---

15. Ireton, *Circle of the Seasons*, 13, 16; Gross, *Christian Year*, 17–22; Chan, *Liturgical Worship*, 164; Johnson, "Worship in Late Antiquity," 77–79.

16. Johnson, "Apostolic Tradition," 60–62.

17. The "Daily Office" (or Opus Dei, "Work of God") or eight hours of prayer in medieval Benedictine abbeys included: Lauds, Prime, Terce, Sext, None, Vespers, Compline, and Vigils. Benedict, *Rule of St. Benedict*, 25–26. "This balance of prayer and work helps to keep us from various prideful temptations." Okholm, *Monk Habits*, 101–4.

Christian remembrance. Evangelicals of free-church Baptist, Pentecostal or Charismatic, and modern nondenominational traditions, owing in part to American Puritan and evangelical revivalist heritage, significantly reduced the days of the calendar even further, retaining perhaps only Christmas Day, Palm Sunday, and Easter Sunday. The larger calendar, which included these and other dates above related to Christ's incarnate life and heavenly ministry, were associated with medieval Roman Catholic legalism. As a result, many Protestant evangelicals end the Resurrection season immediately after Easter Sunday, although Christ continued to appear bodily to his followers for forty more days until the ascension, and for much of Christian history the Day of Pentecost, celebrating the promised Holy Spirit given, has been annually celebrated. Interestingly, the same modern churches that remember Christmas and Easter Week, which lack as much biblical prescription as the other days of the calendar, thereby lack the *liturgical* connection between Christ's incarnation, death, and resurrection with his ascension into heaven and giving of the Holy Spirit to his new temple, the church, until the closure of history. However, more churches today severed from this past seem to be revisiting the benefits of a fuller church calendar, and especially as society moves increasingly toward a more strictly secular approach to life and measure of time.

Some churches also moved toward more republican (Presbyterian) and democratic (Baptist) styles of government, which coincided with the declining affirmation of absolute political monarchies in the seventeenth and eighteenth centuries. Unlike Lutherans and Anglicans, other groups rooted in the Protestant Reformation, like English Calvinist Presbyterians and Methodists, sought to establish more of a middle way between a prescribed ritual order and allowing for new freedoms in a worship service—namely in the form of extemporaneous prayer.[18]

The movements of the Reformation ignited important pathways that engaged and empowered lay people with a greater sense of responsibility and freedom for their spiritual development, including the formation of small groups in German Lutheran colleges of piety, "*ecclesiola in ecclesia*," as well as among the Moravian Brethren and English and American Methodist societies.[19] One of the visions of the Protestant Reformation was putting the word into the hands of the people so that they could realize their own spiritual priesthood and responsibility for growing in their faith and

---

18. Tel, "Calvinist and Reformed Practices," 186, 213–15.
19. Lewis, *Zinzendorf*, 51–52.

obedience in love of God. The Protestant principle of *sola Scriptura* and free readings of the word have contributed much to the vitality of Christianity in the modern era, especially in the United States and globally.[20] It was not the *intention* of the Reformers that this eliminated the need for pastors as well as spiritual counselors, nor did it always mean having to drastically change the traditional liturgical order of Sunday worship.[21]

America's political establishment of religious equality at the beginning of the nineteenth century—affirmed by deists as well as traditional Christians[22]—further allowed for the open and creative development of newer forms of Christian worship. Along with a tradition of English dissent among Baptists, American-born denominations deviated from the highly ceremonial styles of the older churches of Europe, which were perceived as ritualistic, dominated by a clerical class, restrictive of the freedom of Spirit-led worship, lacking in prescriptive biblical authority, and perceived as culturally out of touch with a democratic ethos of individual dignity and empowerment in the expanding young republic. Yet as these new theologically creative and culturally adaptive movements contributed a newer form of personal engagement than older styles, which perhaps helped stall America's drift toward secularism as in Europe, this change was not without its own complications. In a post-Enlightenment world, people tend to view newer change and correction as always better, but in the process, such optimism blinds people to the *problems* of change. New solutions come with new problems. Ignoring what was good about the older forms is often not appreciated until much later after changes have digressed excessively far in the opposite direction.

Although early Lutheran and Calvinist churches of the Protestant Reformation did not entirely do away with every piece of the medieval liturgy altogether, modern evangelical Bible, nondenominational, Baptist, Pentecostal, and charismatic churches often look down on older denominational forms possessing a higher degree of ceremonial, ritual order as culturally out of touch, technologically archaic, and a hangover of unbiblical,

---

20. McGrath, *Christianity's Dangerous Idea*.

21. Pak, "Scripture, the Priesthood," 52–68.

22. Diversity of interpretations in Reformation Europe devolved into a host of competing institutional and popular divisions that, combined with government oppression and war, turned many early modern minds to favor a religion of rational monotheism. While in America, organized religion was still encouraged among the masses, in some cases like France, there was a more aggressive secularization of society. Gregory, *Unintended Reformation*, 129–79.

medieval Roman Catholicism.²³ As a result, many popular church services today have been simplified (or eroded) to a collection of praise and worship songs, a brief prayer, a lengthy and topically motivational sermon derived from Scripture, and an altar call. Melanie Ross argues that this was significantly begun with the influence of nineteenth-century New York revival preacher Charles Finney, whose Arminian theology of universal human empowerment (not the closed, secret divine election of Calvinists), coupled to the new-world, American context of experimental freedom, adapted "new measures" like the anxious bench. Outdoor revival meetings were designed to engage and motivate people to counter the spiritual apathy and ineffective ministry Finney blamed on the older brick-and-mortar liturgical forms.²⁴

An interesting but often ignored chapter in the history of North American Christianity is the rise, especially in the twentieth century, of Messianic Judaism. Congregations of Jewish Christians were formed to preserve a historical and cultural connection to their Hebrew heritage and the first-synagogue Christians, rejecting assimilation to forms of worship shaped more exclusively by centuries of gentile predominance over the churches (often including a spirit of anti-Semitism masked by a strict replacement theology). Whereas high-charismatic and high-liturgical forms of worship are most often viewed as diametrically incompatible in the churches of Protestantism and Roman Catholicism, Messianic Judaism offers a unique blending of traditional liturgy (Hebrew Shabbat prayers, lectionary readings from the Torah), the keeping of annual Jewish feast days imparted with their New Covenant fulfillment in Yeshua (Passover, Yom Kippur, Pentecost), lively Davidic folk dance, and more spontaneous expressions of prayer and charismatic experiences of the work of *Ruach HaKodesh* (Holy Spirit) in prophesying and healing.²⁵

Several decades ago, as contemporary worship became vogue, a movement among younger, dissatisfied free-church Protestant evangelicals was turning back towards the older, high-liturgical denominations—particularly Anglican.²⁶ These worship services often move more slowly, are

---

23. Ruth and Lim, *Praise and Worship*, 261–69. For a recent argument for high liturgical forms by a member of the Mennonite free-church tradition, see Rempel, *Recapturing an Enchanted World*.

24. Ross, "Evangelical Practices of Worship," 256–59.

25. See Rudolph, "Messianic Judaism," 25–30; Klayman, "Messianic Jewish Worship" 51–59.

26. Webber and Ruth, *Evangelicals on the Canterbury Trail*.

quieter, more somber, reflective, and reverent, and much of the service is prescribed in formal responsory prayers, recitation of creeds and readings from Scripture, and annual cycles of sermon texts. These younger evangelicals, born into contemporary styles of worship, recognized a disconnection from the church's liturgical history and its benefits. First of all, the older form of liturgy provided an experience of continuity with Christian worshippers through past ages and a historical anchoring and rootedness that was not subject to the whims and fads of cultural change. Many were also seeking a form of worship and Christianity that expressed a deeper sense of awe, beauty, and reverence, as they witnessed modern attempts of churches to over-contextualize and, in the name of relevance, marketed worship services to attract the consumer-entertainment tastes of American pop culture.

Even the most casual, emotionally expressive, and less ceremonial forms of worship today cannot avoid incorporating a "ritual of primal simplicity,"[27] including the ritual of when and where to meet and a church order that generally includes a common pattern of singing, prayers, and a lesson from Scripture. For all their novelty and creativity to keep pace with modern culture, Christian churches of most every stripe follow a "basic *ordo*," or liturgy, that has remained essentially constant throughout history.[28] Later churches from the Reformation on may have reduced the amount of ceremony in worship over valid concerns of ritualism and in attempts to become more "biblical" and like the New Testament, but the most primitive ritual structure of ancient Christian worship remains in song, prayer, proclamation, offering, and (even if occasional) communion.

During the recent pandemic, many Christians realized how much more important was the simple ritual of meeting weekly in person for worship when suddenly they were urged to lock down and quarantine. Worshiping together via the internet may have been a necessary (but poor) substitute for a season, but it revealed that loving God in the ritual of worship (*storge*) and in the real presence of others ran much deeper than many took for granted. A feeling of nostalgia toward familiar church liturgy brought a certain joy to the character Aleksandr Petrovich exiled in Siberia

---

27. Rempel, *Recapturing an Enchanted World*, 33, 38.

28. Chan, *Liturgical Theology*, 50, 62. Indeed, Ruth and Lim describe the 1990s contemporary praise and worship movement using new musical styles with evangelistic intentions as the "new liturgical normal." Ruth and Lim, *Praise and Worship*, 291–93.

when he and other prisoners were allowed to attend church services during the Lenten season.[29]

The Benefits and Limits of Liturgical *Storge*

The reality is that whatever the structure and form worshiping communities take—from the older, complex, and elaborate to the newer, simpler, and minimalist—through repetition of practice and experience, these traditions and habits steadily form an identity and even more importantly, a theology, and often subtly beyond perception. Echoing the language of early church fathers such as Origen, Augustine, and Cyprian, the sixteenth-century Swiss Reformer John Calvin described the organized visible church as our "Mother" "into whose bosom God is pleased to gather his sons . . . that they may be guided by her motherly care until they mature and at last reach the goal of faith . . . for those to whom he is Father the church may also be Mother."[30] Some ancient Christian communities even constructed baptismal fonts like female reproductive organs to graphically symbolize a new birth from the womb of baptism into a new family to be formed through communal participation in the worshiping church.[31]

Tish Harrison Warren, in her popular book *Liturgy of the Ordinary*, makes a convincing case that we live life in rituals every day. In fact, non-cognitive or subconscious habits and patterns (rituals) shape most of our lives. Warren provides the analogy of driving a car: how complicated would it be if every time people got behind the wheel, they had to think through every step like it was their first time? She also shares how her own morning routine of reaching for her smartphone had become an unhealthy ritual, which betrayed an attachment and addiction, feeding her first waking thoughts with self-entitlement through codependency on technology. "By reaching for my smartphone every morning, I had developed a ritual that trained me toward a certain end: entertainment and stimulation via

---

29. Dostoyevsky, *House of the Dead*, 274–75. This book fictionalizes Dostoyevsky's own time in a Siberian labor camp between 1850 and 1854.

30. "For there is no other way to enter into life unless this mother conceive us in her womb, give us birth, nourish us at her breast, and lastly, unless she keep us under her care and guidance." Calvin, *Institutes*, 1013–16; Lubac, *Motherhood of the Church*, 47–58.

31. Jenson, "Baptismal Rites and Architecture," 139 (and Plate E).

technology ... my unexamined daily habit was shaping me into a worshiper of glowing screens."[32]

James Smith describes humans as "liturgical animals," in that so much of life is noncognitive behaviors built through repetition and practice. (As I type the manuscript of this book, I am thankful for keyboarding lessons in grade school which, through ritual and practice, trained my muscle memory so that I can type different keys rapidly without thinking about each of them.) In words reminiscent of Lewis's description of how *storge* develops in human affection, Smith describes formation in social liturgies as "a communal, collective disposition that gets inscribed in me ... a handed-down way of being ... something that comes *to* me, from outside me." Habits of thinking and acting formed within community are infused below the level of "rational deliberation or conscious awareness," and because of that, they have the power to produce and shape in ways unseen, taken for granted as if "natural" and "second nature."[33]

Aren't rituals, habits, and disciplines[34] good for human bodies? Habits are helpful when feelings and motivations are lacking, such as in eating well and exercise. The more a habit is sustained, feelings and motivations will often follow. On the other hand, the longer a good habit is avoided, the harder it is to *feel* like starting it (or picking it up again), and in the meantime the space is open for poor habits to take their place. (If I must snack, is it my habit to grab something caloric and processed or something natural and healthy?) If Warren and Smith are right, that humans are by nature creatures of habit, then the question becomes not *whether* life is embodied in rituals, but in *what* habits and rituals, and *how* do they form us.

What about habits and rituals of faith or spiritual life? The common argument against ritual when it comes to Christian worship is that, while these may engage the body they also—like the routine of driving or typing—become disconnected from the mind and spirit (ever get lost in thought while driving the same route home?). Christians today, however, seek an

---

32. Warren, *Liturgy of the Ordinary*, 31. James Smith refers to this as the "iPhoneization" and "deformation" of our worldview. Contrary to popular thinking, and like forms of worship, the medium of digital technology is not inherently neutral and only dependent upon the intent of the user. See *Imagining the Kingdom*, 141–45, 148, 168–69.

33. Smith, *Imagining the Kingdom*, 81–83, 140; Smith, *You Are What You Love*, 29, 32–38.

34. Throughout this chapter, I am using the terms "habits", "rituals", and "traditions" interchangeably as practices performed repeatedly and consistently, particularly with the liturgical context of worshiping communities in view.

experience of worship that fully engages the individual—body, mind, and soul (emotions). Just as Lewis warns about affection (*storge*) within human relationships,[35] is an affection for God developed through rituals and habits of Christian worship subject to a *spiritual* malaise and indifference, maybe even a contempt toward familiarity? German liberal church historian Adolf von Harnack argued that all originally dynamic spiritual movements tend to ossify over time into more structured forms that depersonalize (and pervert) the gospel of God's relationship to each individual soul.[36]

It is customary among many Christians today to think negatively of anything that is habitual or that lacks strong personal emotion as inauthentic and, therefore, displeasing to God. "Protestants do not usually go for the habitual when it comes to spirituality. For some reason we grow up with the bias that spiritual practice is 'real' only if it is spontaneous. Habits . . . strike us as fake spirituality."[37] It was partly an excessive liturgical devotion (*storge*) that lacked personal spiritual desire (*eros*) and moral action (*philia*) that inspired eighteenth-century movements of Pietism in Lutheran Germany and British evangelical revivalism in Anglican England.

It was also political and social division over precision in liturgical (and doctrinal) matters among Catholic and Protestant churches that led to the rise of more radical Spiritualist Anabaptist groups and the origin of the Society of Friends (or Quakers) who so emphasized the inward personal desire for God (*eros*) to the point of diminishing or eliminating Christian liturgical worship (*storge*) altogether.

This same division also appeared to justify for many intellectuals the response of seventeenth-century Enlightenment deism against organized religion, severing reason and morality from both the liturgical worship of the church (*storge*) and the resources of Christian spiritual experience (*eros*). The death of God, or secular, theologies of the 1960s similarly emphasized the active moral life (*philia*), excluding the need for any spiritual formation in the church's liturgy (*storge*) or the spiritual desire of contemplative prayer (*eros*): "That man is not to become fascinated with God Himself. . . .

---

35. For Lewis, this indifference and apathy to Anglican churchgoing was a reason for his creation of the imaginative world of Narnia, to reawaken modern English people to the marvels of the Christian worldview from the outside. Lewis also states that the modern skeptic must be combated by other ways than mere direct, rational apologetics, but lining other sorts of literature with a "latent" Christian worldview. Lewis, "Christian Apologetics," in *God in the Dock*, 93.

36. Harnack, *What Is Christianity*, 198–99, 238, 242, 263.

37. Okholm, *Monk Habits*, 21–22.

Rather than shutting out the world to delve into each other's depths the way adolescent lovers do, God and man find joy together in a common task.... God wants man to be interested not in Him but in his fellow man."[38]

Relying on *storge* alone in human loves can "go bad on us."[39] When it comes to Christian liturgy, our love for God can also be diminished by a focus on *storge* alone: "Without meaningful participation, a liturgical practice is quickly turned into mere ritualism," says Simon Chan. At the same time, "the problem may have more to do with the attitude of the worshiper than with the liturgy itself. What for one is drab sameness may be for another welcome familiarity."[40]

It is a prejudiced caricature to insinuate that the sincere devotion of the heart can only coexist with the lowest liturgical forms of worship. Many Christians today assume that only freer, more spontaneous, culturally relevant, and emotionally charged forms of worship—set to modern folk/pop/R&B/rock music—equate to spiritual authenticity. First, how has emotional fulfillment and expressiveness come to mean so much more in Christian worship than respect and reverence? In other words, do people come to church foremost to feel something or to revere Someone?[41] Also, this assumption that pits a greater degree of liturgical ceremony against heart religion was challenged by the case of the Wesley brothers, who for all their Methodist revival emphasis on the importance of experiencing a personal relationship with Christ in the heart urged faithful participation in the Anglican liturgy—especially the weekly practice of communion.[42]

In the late 1900s, younger denominational and nondenominational church movements, in the noble efforts to reach unchurched people,

---

38. Cox, *Secular City*, 264–65. Like Cox, Robinson views Christianity for the modern world as not requiring a turning away as individuals or groups from the world to meet with a personal God in heaven (i.e., in prayer and worship), but a full turning and immersion in the world for others. In enveloping the sacred fully within the secular, Robinson's Jesus is shorn of any supernatural status, liturgy and worship have nothing to do with communing with a personal God beyond the world and history, and morality is only concerned with human love and relationships. Robinson, *Honest to God*, 61, 68, 86–88, 97, 99–101, 105, 116–19.

39. Lewis, *Four Loves*, 34, 35.

40. Chan, *Liturgical Theology*, 151.

41. See also chapter 3's discussion of *eros* and individualism in contemporary worship.

42. The Wesleys celebrated communion weekly and viewed the ritual as "an occasion of heightened expectation of a deep spiritual encounter." One of the Wesleys' communion hymns speaks of "the fire of love" and the impartation of Christ's life and power to hearts of faith in the celebration. Chan, *Liturgical Theology*, 95.

completely discarded any semblance of older, more reverent and regal forms of worship to accommodate the more casual, consumerist social spirit of modern movie theaters and concert venues. Many churches adapted their worship services in the 80s without considering how these updated forms might end up reinforcing the cultural mindset of self-absorbed, consumer-minded, and entertainment-obsessed individuals. Rather than impressing the worship service as the place of God's gracious invitation to gathered Christians to find their true humanity in reverent submission to his desires, God was often invited to come and bless the desires of the people—a baptized form of egocentrism, emotional hedonism, and technological dependence.[43]

Many churches, claiming to be "Bible based," have not only removed the recitation of ancient creeds but also the historically central role of the public reading of Scripture and assume they are being more faithful to Jesus by celebrating the Lord's Supper *less* frequently than he instructed.[44] Many evangelicals justify this by suggesting that the bread and wine (or grape juice!) are *mere* symbols, and they wish to avoid the empty ritualism and superstitious abuses of the medieval Roman Catholic Mass that treated it like harnessing magic. Yet this has also led to an excessive dualism that depreciates the Lord's Supper and its ability as a visual, symbolic portrayal to remind Christians that the door to worship God in the heavenly courts was opened and remains opened to sinners through the sacrifice of Christ. It fails to appreciate how God *can* communicate himself to us analogically and symbolically through the physical world to awaken and nourish faith by repeated, sensory experience of transcendent truth.[45] There is an

---

43. I am often puzzled by efforts to make church services as aesthetically comfortable and attractive as possible to suit popular preferences, while it is communicated from the pulpit that Christians are to *die to self* and lay down their lives, even in suffering, for Christ and others.

44. "In the same way, after supper He took the cup, saying, 'This cup is the new covenant in my blood; do this, whenever you drink it, in remembrance of me.' For as often as you eat this bread and drink the cup, you proclaim the Lord's death until He comes." 1 Cor 11:25–26.

45. Lewis's upbringing in Anglicanism and his interest in the medieval worldview enabled him to appreciate the communication of truth through symbolical signs. A master of analogy, his whole creation of Narnia was to serve as a symbolic myth that awakened imagination to the truth and reality of the Christian story. In fact, in *The Last Battle*, we learn that Narnia is but the "Shadowlands" of "a more real and more beautiful Narnia," the home of Aslan, much like Lewis viewed the world we know as but a shadow of heaven (and hell). Lewis, *Last Battle*, 761–67. "The blessed will say, 'We have never lived anywhere except in Heaven,' and the Lost, 'We were always in Hell.'" Lewis, *Great*

important but often confused difference between believing that God *can use* consecrated objects and rituals as bridges between the physical and the spiritual and viewing God's presence and power as *subject, bound,* or *wholly contained* in them to be manipulated.[46] He is at once both transcendent and immanent (Acts 17:24–28).[47] He is not only at work and reveals himself when bypassing or suspending the natural order in miracles but also as he works and reveals himself *through* the miracle of the natural order itself. He not only can touch the soul directly by his Spirit but also through the outward agency of human language and creativity in sermon and song. For younger evangelicals to accuse older regal forms of worship having large amounts of ceremonial ritual as "man-made" is to underestimate how much modern forms with less ceremony are as well, including the songs chosen and the design (and rehearsal!) of the musical arrangements. The human and physical character of Christian worship, regardless of the form or style, cannot be entirely avoided, even by those that claim to adhere to the New Testament and freedom of the Spirit most strictly. Every cultural form of liturgy, whether the heavily prescribed, regal, and reverent, or the laid-back, theatrical, and emotionally expressive, is corruptible by becoming excessive.

The Old Testament does speak plentifully against empty liturgical performance (Isa 29:13; Ps 51:16; 1 Sam 15:22; Hos 6:6; Mic 6:6–8). Jesus echoes the prophetic tradition that expressed God's disgust for Israel's empty offerings (Isa 1:13). He also challenged man-made traditions that had come to rival God's commandments. Yet, Jesus also did not discourage people from observing the Torah rituals of synagogue and temple. His primary concern was that Pharisaical interpretations and outward ceremonial worship was neglecting, excluding, or hindering obedience to the explicit commandments of God in "weightier matters" of justice and mercy (Matt 23:23, NKJV). His censure was less an attack on their lack of enthusiasm,

---

Divorce, in *Signature Classics*, 503.

46. Rempel, *Recapturing an Enchanted World*, 19, 23, 96–97.

47. Paul in Athens was preaching to a crowd including Stoics and Epicureans, who disagreed about the nature of divine being in relationship to the material cosmos. Stoics stressed divine immanence (see 17:28), and Epicureans stressed divine transcendence. This rational quandary came up again in the philosophy of the Enlightenment, including Baruch Spinoza (1632–77) who viewed "God" monistically as the whole of nature and one material substance ("the indwelling spirit of an impersonal order"), and deism, which separated God from repeated interventionist engagement and dynamic response within the process of the material world. Taylor, *Secular Age*, 274–75, 280.

passion, and emotional desire for God (*eros*). Paul described them as not lacking in zeal for God (Rom 10). An over-Romanticized evangelical Christianity today equates feelings with authenticity, but Jesus was more concerned with how their proud satisfaction of loving God with *storge* ultimately blocked their view of the full heart of God's kingdom (*philia*)—his active generosity, compassion, and merciful love toward all Jews (and all mankind) as sinners.

Storge does need the other loves to complete it and to prevent it from becoming a spiritually moribund and morally complacent ritualism. To narrow or exclude loving God to *storge*, whatever form it takes, thereby diminishes it. Yes, loving God should involve personal desire for him (*eros*), but it should also extend beyond the assembled worshiping church into the world in likeness to the suffering ministry of Christ for the sake of the kingdom (*philia*).[48] In this sense, it can rightly be said that "we worship *for* mission" and "we gather *for* sending."[49]

Lewis suggests that the love of *storge* also adds color to what is lacking in the other loves day to day. "They would not perhaps wear very well without it."[50] What is particularly important for this discussion is its durability established through time. What is seen as a possible weakness, building affection for God through the repetition and familiarity of Christian liturgy, is also its greatest strength and most unique contribution to the other loves. It may not always manifest in a thrilling emotional experience of *eros* or appear as noble as the sacrificial moral heroism of *philia*, but the fact that *storge* becomes like second nature through habit means that it can also be the most durable, as Lewis observes regarding the growth and endurance of familial affection.

Christians who rely too much on feelings and emotions, fleeting as they are, will be disappointed and disillusioned. Lewis warned against expecting emotions to always accompany attendance to worship services as well as spiritual disciplines of prayer and Bible reading. He viewed these as a matter of duty and disciplined obedience that God will continue to use whether he chooses to awaken strong feelings in us or not.[51] Like rain that

---

48. God's mission from Genesis to Revelation, with an inaugurated fulfillment in Christ and his body (the church), is that one day all of creation will become one sanctuary united with his full and perfect presence. Beale and Kim, *God Dwells among Us*.

49. Smith, *Imagining the Kingdom*, 15; Schmemann, *Life of the World*, 137.

50. Lewis, *Four Loves*, 34, 35.

51. Downing, *Region of Awe*, 159–61. Lewis practiced what he preached in his attendance to weekly Anglican services and personal devotion in Bible reading and praying

cannot always be depended upon, rituals and habits of Christian worship are like the roots that nourish a tree not only in the fruit-bearing spring and summer but also sustain its life through the cold and dreary months of fall and winter. Throughout the centuries, Christians have gathered collectively to express love for God by sharing in the habits of liturgical worship, including a common core of prayers, songs, and the nurturing of faith through word and sacrament. Whether Lutheran, Presbyterian, Roman Catholic, Baptist, Pentecostal, Orthodox, or other, the content and form of this core should orient people toward God in spirit and truth against any "rival *telos*." This especially includes today's "secular liturgies" that "functionally tell the story that *I* am the center of the universe; that the world—and perhaps even God—exist for my pleasure . . . a kind of centripetal force tending toward *me* at the center."[52] In essence, loving God through the familiarity of liturgical worship—affection or *storge*—should also be a love to God that grows in abiding personal desire for God (*eros*) and is expressed in friendship with Christ (*philia*) on a mission of sacrificial service for the world.

---

through the Psalter in the Book of Common Prayer. Dorsett, "Lewis and Care of Souls."

52. Smith, *Imagining the Kingdom*, 123, 140.

2

Philia

Loving God in Friendship with Christ

WHAT LEWIS CALLS THE least necessary of the human loves, friendship (*philia*), has received minimal attention in modern thought. Biological necessity and the spirit of Romanticism have given the love of family and the love between the sexes center stage in the history of sacred and secular literature: "Without *Eros* none of us would have been begotten and without Affection none of us would have been reared; but we can live and breed without friendship. The species, biologically considered, has no need of it."[1]

Yet, it was friendship love that was extolled by ancient writers like Aristotle and Cicero as the chief of all loves, and it was also the one favored by medieval ascetics who shunned the traditional domestic attachments of family and marriage to live as brothers in monastic communities (or as sisters in convents).

Unlike *storge* that grows with those we happen to be around for a given time, and even the irresistible impulses of *eros*, Lewis says our friendships are loves chosen by us. They subdivide our connections to the broader community of social relationships into smaller, more intimate units. "To say 'These are my friends' implies 'Those are not.'"[2]

---

1. Lewis, *Four Loves*, 58.

2. Lewis, *Four Loves*, 60. Consider how social media today allows us to choose who our "friends" are, and even within that generic circle we can control what some friends see and others don't, as our closer friends are allowed to peer deeper into our digital lives

Although friendship love can grow out of or into erotic desire (and Lewis challenges the association of "firm and serious" friendship between the common sexes as necessarily homosexual), the two types of love bear important distinctions. For Lewis, the essence of *philia* arises when two or more "companions" who share a "common religion, common studies, a common profession, even a common recreation," realize they share an even deeper union of perspective, concern, or vision for the world and the truth even to the point of adding to the fullness of what each person sees or experiences individually. It is the moment when we say, "You too? I thought I was the only one!" *Eros*, for Lewis, has two lovers lost in each other's gaze, but *philia* has two or more looking out toward the world shoulder-to-shoulder: "The very condition of having Friends is that we should want something else besides Friends. . . . Friendship must be about something even if it were only an enthusiasm for dominoes or white mice."[3]

Lewis says that friendships are not necessarily exclusive between two individuals, but since the friendship exists because of something other than the friendship, they are more naturally open to widening the circle to receive others. While superficial companionship is more possible between a larger group, "friendship" exists at a deeper level between two to four people who see and care about the same truth: "The man who agrees with us that some question, little regarded by others, is of great importance can be our Friend. He need not agree with us about the answer."[4] Lewis's own circle of Oxford friends and creative writing group, the Inklings—including J. R. R. Tolkien, Owen Barfield, Charles Williams, Warren Lewis, and others—was likely in mind when Lewis framed his definition of friendship.[5]

While not necessary to our propagation and survival, Lewis extols friendship love for adding "practical" or "civilization value" to human life and history. Lewis agrees with Aristotle and Cicero who defined friendship as providing mutual admiration and support. In the *Nichomachean Ethics*, Aristotle describes friendship as "one of the most indispensable requirements of life . . . the happy man requires friends."[6] He distinguishes a lower form of friendship in utility, based on an exchange of some advantage or benefit in aristocratic patronage or employment; a friendship of pleasure,

---

than others.

3. Lewis, *Four Loves*, 66.
4. Lewis, *Four Loves*, 60–66.
5. Glyer, *Bandersnatch*, 121–22.
6. Aristotle, *Nichomachean Ethics*, 205.

wherein friends love each other for the pleasure they feel in each other's company; and lastly, the most permanent kind, a friendship based on the mutual admiration of virtue and goodwill, consisting more in giving honor than receiving it. Friendships such as the latter, Aristotle says, are both the means to, and the ends of, a strong and just State. Similarly, the Latin rhetorician Cicero of the first century BC wrote a treatise devoted to friendship (in Latin *amicitia*, which shares the root word of "amor," or love).

Like the Greeks, Cicero considers friendship the greatest of loves: "For nothing we have from the gods is better or more enjoyable than friendship. . . . Even if someone has all the riches fortune can give, a life without the joys of friendship is empty and miserable."[7] Cicero echoes many thoughts of Aristotle on the advantages of friendship, especially between the good and virtuous, and dwells on the mutual good will, affection, and sharing of interests, opinions, and moral values that draws certain friends together and adds brightness to their joys and eases their sorrows. A few centuries later, the Christian bishop of North Africa, Augustine, described the blessings of friendship with classical overtones.[8]

Lewis partially agrees with these definitions but with an important nuance: "The common quest or vision which unites Friends does not absorb them in such a way that they remain ignorant or oblivious of one another. . . . One knows nobody so well as one's 'fellow.'"[9] However, for Lewis this mutual care is but accidental to what the friendship is ultimately defined by—"the common quest." He observes how such friendships are behind the birth of significant world-changing movements: "Friendship is both a possible benefactor and a possible danger to the community." The Romantic movement, Communism, Methodism, anti-slavery movements, the Renaissance, the Protestant Reformation, "might perhaps be said, without much exaggeration, to have begun in the same way." These movements started with a common attitude toward the world. They were willing to "turn their backs" and secede, a growing and powerful flame for the truth they saw together. Early Christians banded together against their world, but the same could be said of "criminals, cranks, or perverts." Friendship may be a rebellion "of good men against the badness of society or of bad men

---

7. Cicero, *How to Be a Friend*, 101.

8. Lewis was critical of Augustine for seeming to disparage the ties of friendship elsewhere. Lewis, *Four Loves*, 120–21. This was a mistaken interpretation by Lewis, and the two essentially agreed upon the value of earthly friendships as well as that all human attachments must not disturb or come between love of God. Hansen, "Friendship," 19–30.

9. Lewis, *Four Loves*, 68–71.

against its goodness. . . . Friendship (as the ancients saw) can be a school of virtue; but also (as they did not see) a school of vice. It is ambivalent. It makes good men better and bad men worse." By its very nature exclusionary, and in deafness to voices outside that may be justified and necessary, therein lies the demon of friendship when it morphs into a "wholesale indifference or deafness" and a prideful and aristocratic-like elitism.[10]

Lewis states that *philia* is the poorest image of symbolizing human fellowship with God. *Storge* and *eros* are readily found in Scripture, from God as "Father" to Christ as "Bridegroom," but friendship is "rarely" though "not entirely neglected." Lewis suggests that this is for the best and likely intentional since this image could be mistakenly conveyed for reality, leading to a false sense of equality with almighty God.[11] This is one of the few times in *The Four Loves* that Lewis develops an explicit connection between the image of human love with its divine archetype, and this negatively. Is there a way to be faithful to Lewis and Scripture in developing friendship (*philia*) with God as a faithful form of Christian love?[12]

Philia: Friendship with Christ

It seems that when Christians today speak of being the friend of Christ, most often they have in mind the consoling presence of the Lord. For example, the well-known hymn "What a Friend We Have in Jesus" (1855) defines friendship with Christ in terms of his faithfulness in comforting our sorrows and griefs:

> Have we trials and temptations?
> Is there trouble anywhere?
> We should never be discouraged;
> Take it to the Lord in prayer!
> Can we find a friend so faithful
> Who will all our sorrows share?
> Jesus knows our every weakness;
> Take it to the Lord in prayer![13]

---

10. Lewis, *Four Loves*, 68–69, 80–83, 86–87.

11. Lewis, *Four Loves*, 78, 87–88. Plato rejected the idea of friendship with God on account of God, being by nature perfect *apatheia*, cannot truly and mutually love humankind in return. Moltmann, *Crucified God*, 268.

12. Such as described by Leiva-Merikakis, *Love's Sacred Order*, 84–85.

13. Scriven, "What a Friend," 261.

Jesus does invite his followers to cast their wearisome burdens upon him (Matt 11:28–30), but what does it look like to be a friend *to Jesus*? Is friendship with Christ the lower kind described by Aristotle, one of utility (a one-sided benefit or advantage) or an emotional pleasure gained from his presence?

Abraham was described as a "friend of God" (Isa 41:8; Jas 2:23 KJV), and Moses spoke to God face to face "as a man speaks to his friend" (Exod 33:11). Jesus called the apostles his "friends" (John 15:5), spending most of his time with them, welcoming them into his intimate inner circle, giving them the interpretation of his parables, and revealing to them the mind and will of the Father for the kingdom. Then, he sent them out to serve his kingdom-building ministry in the power of the Spirit. Their friendship with each other involved a love of good will and mutual support (John 13:34), and Jesus also promised his continuing presence through his words and the Holy Spirit (John 16:7; Matt 20:20), but their friendship with Jesus and each other existed because of the mission and the quest they were chosen for in his name. Indeed, apart from those who were related, what likelihood would these men have found to associate together including a tax collector? What defined their friendship *to Jesus* was sharing his view of truth, his intimacy with the Father, and the heart of his redemptive mission in the world: "You are my friends if you do what I command" (John 15:14). With that friendship came the expectation of following his way of sacrificial suffering for others and the peaceable building of his kingdom, forgiving as he forgives, showing mercy as he shows mercy, loving as he loved in patience and generosity, even at great cost, in loss or pain. To be a friend of God, therefore, is to have "the mind of Christ" (1 Cor 2:16). Friendship *to* Jesus would not preserve them from distress and troubles but rather they would join themselves to him on the same path (John 16:33). Conformity to the mind and life of Christ in obedience through suffering is, for Paul, the very reason for which Christians have been chosen, called, and saved *in* this world (Rom 8:29–30). Thus, friendship (*philia*) with Jesus is a significant manifestation of loving God in the Christian life. It is the most important friendship and one that allows for no loves to rival (Luke 14:26).

The disciples of Jesus would not be able to consider themselves his friends if they chose to live by the idolatrous principles of the world, for "friendship with the world means enmity with God" (Jas 4:4). Rebellion against the sovereignty of God and to grasp on to life as *my own* to live is to be a friend of the devil, who took Adam and Eve down with him to share in the judgment upon his vanity, pride, and lust to rival God in freedom and independence. Promises of a better life and playing on the desire for nobility of self were precisely the deceptive ploys of the "Un-man" in Lewis's novel *Perelandra* (1945). The innocent woman on the planet Venus was told by the interplanetary visitor (falsely) that it was the will of her Creator (Maleldil) that his creation grows up to be free and independent of him:

> "He longs—oh, how greatly He longs—to see His creature become fully itself, to stand up in its own reason and its own courage even against Him. . . . Do you think He is not weary of seeing nothing but Himself in all that He has made? If that contented Him, why should He create at all? To find the Other—the thing whose will is no longer His—that is Maleldil's desire." . . . Progress passed before his [Ransom's] eyes in a great momentary vision: cities, armies, tall ships, and libraries and fame, and the grandeur of poetry spurting like a fountain out of the labors and ambitions of men. Who could be certain that Creative Evolution was not the deepest truth? . . . What the Un-man said was always very nearly true. Certainly it must be part of the Divine plan that this happy creature should mature, should become more and more a creature of free choice, should become, in a sense, more distinct from God and from her husband in order thereby to be at one with them in a richer fashion.[14]

For some nineteenth-century Romantic authors, God was even viewed as the enemy and tyrant of humanity, and the heroic devil of Milton's *Paradise Lost* symbolized the spirit of human liberation and progress, unlimited pursuit of enlightenment, freedom, and mastery of nature.[15] Cain, likewise, is extended some sympathy by the Romantic poet Lord Byron in wrestling with the justice of God in human suffering and death caused by Adam and Eve's natural curiosity and desire to increase in knowledge: "What have we done that we must be victims for a deed before our birth, or need victims to atone for this mysterious, nameless sin, if it be such a sin to seek for knowledge?"[16]

Like the covetous aspirations of Adam and Eve to desire more than what God intended for them as his creatures, however, greed for knowledge

---

14. Lewis, *Perelandra*, 101, 104, 114.

15. Russell, *Prince of Darkness*, 220–27; Camus, *Rebel*, 47–48.

16. Steffan, *Lord Byron's Cain*, 232–33. Lord Byron apparently claimed that his work was purely an exploratory literary work and not meant to convey his own religious perspective, but conservative and liberal critics thought otherwise. See 11, 455–58.

and freedom did not bring the life they thought they were missing, but rather destroyed the life they already had but defiantly and shamefully squandered. The problems of the human condition in envy, hate, and violence have not been cured by time, knowledge and education, political and social change, and economic consumption.[17] ("Hell and destruction are never full; so the eyes of man are never satisfied," Prov 27:20 KJV.) Even centuries of religious reform have not resolved the fundamental human predicament. Sadly, historical Christianity has often been more tempted by the alluring desire for power and wealth, aligning with oppressive structures and, in the name of virtue, committing the foulest deeds against humanity.

Friendship with Christ (*philia*) is to share in the vision of "a common quest."[18] To share the mind of Christ is to view the Father, the world, and the meaning of human life the way Jesus saw it and lived it, not as something to be greedily consumed or exploited for the privilege of the few to the exclusion of others, not as something whose dominion is measured by promises of technological efficiency or the proud comforts accumulated in material prosperity. Friendship with Christ is to ascend by descent through humility, to honor rather than be honored, to serve in kindness, mercy, and love, to pursue the crown of glory through sacrifices of suffering. Friendship with Christ is an active life in and for the world, to love the world through self-giving as God "so loved the world" and *gave* his own son (John 3:16). In the words of Luther, just as a healthy tree produces healthy fruit, so good works do not make the Christian, but a true Christian—in so far as he or she lives in his or her faith, the gift of the Spirit—will do good works.[19]

There have been countless numbers of men and women through the centuries who have exemplified friendship (*philia*) with Christ, who have loved the way God loves and despised what God despises, seeing the truth of the world from God's view. This includes millions of anonymous Christians who in self-denial and in less publicly memorable ways have exhibited remarkable humility, mercy, kindness, and sacrifice in the face of evil toward humanity: "Friendship between a person and God values the mutual

---

17. Myers, *American Paradox*.

18. A recent work written for pastors looks at the classical Greek writings on friendship as well as a Christian perspective in Augustine and Aquinas, but it unforgivably leaves out any reference at all to Lewis's definition of *philia* in *The Four Loves*, neither does it significantly draw out or develop this idea of friendship with Christ as the "common quest" or active mission to the world. Austin, *Friendship*.

19. Luther, *Freedom of a Christian*, 514–15.

concerns of the well-being of the earth and the redemption of humanity."[20] Even when the way of righteousness led to persecution or called for sacrificial hardships, they expressed their love to God by carrying their crosses in imitation of Jesus. They laid down their lives in likeness and obedience to him, and what greater love can you show to a friend (John 15:13)? The same Jesus who needs nothing, and to whom all things have been given, also says, "Whatever you did for the least of these brothers and sisters of mine, you did for me" (Matt 25:40).

Christians demonstrated friendship with Christ not only through the evangelistic ministry of the spoken word, which included calling people to repentance for hypocrisy, greed, and injustice, but also in stewarding their lives sacrificially in love for others. This chapter looks at representative examples of *philia* in Christian history, especially in demonstrating the way of loving God in the active life devoted to ministries of compassion and justice.

Ancient and Medieval Compassion

In the early centuries of Christianity, churches established diaconates, such as in Rome, to serve the widowed, orphaned, and poor populations. During times of spreading epidemic, such as in North Africa in the middle of the third century, Christians were known to risk their lives to care not only for members of their churches but for abandoned pagan neighbors as well before the watchful (and critical) eye of pagan Roman emperors. Greek Christians of fourth-century Byzantium developed *xenodochia* ("hospitality to the stranger"), which were special houses devoted to caring for lepers and the sickly poor. Basil, bishop of Caesarea, believed the express purpose for establishing monastic institutions was to care for the sick and needy. Historians identify these as roots of the modern hospital, having influenced the development of similar houses and charitable orders elsewhere throughout medieval Europe.[21]

Basil also preached vigorously against the proud and luxurious living of wealthy Christians to the neglect of the poor with words that can sting the heart of the comfortable classes today. He called for Christians to model

---

20. Gaddy, *Love Affair with God*, 52.

21. Lynn, *Christian Compassion*, 36–45, 63–66. The first hospital in Rome was established by a wealthy Roman woman named Fabiola. Armstrong, *Medieval Wisdom*, 123–33.

their lives after the simplicity of Jesus, to heed his warnings about the desire for wealth, and to honor the radical devotion of the New Testament church: "Those who love their neighbor as themselves possess nothing more than their neighbor; yet surely you seem to have great possessions! How else can this be, but that you may have preferred your own enjoyment to the consolation of the many? For the more you abound in wealth, the more you lack in love."[22]

Basil's scathing indictment and warning was echoed a few centuries later in a series of sermons on Lazarus and the rich man (Luke 16:19–31) preached by John Chrysostom, who at the time was a priest in Antioch but was soon to become the Bishop of Constantinople. Like Basil, he was an outspoken prophet against the luxuries of the rich: "This also is theft, not to share one's possessions . . . the failure to share one's own goods with others is theft and swindle and defraudation. . . . If you are affluent, but spend more than you need, you will give an account of the funds which were entrusted to you. . . . For you have obtained more than others have, and you have received it, not to spend it for yourself, but to become a good steward for others as well."[23]

By the Middle Ages, in response to the church's wealth, many were now *choosing* a life of poverty in monasteries and convents that dotted the landscape of Western and Eastern Christendom. Poverty was viewed as better for the piety of the individual soul than to have wealth that made one morally weak and corrupted. The path of voluntary suffering, discipline, and self-restraint—in likeness to the witness of the ancient martyrs—was intended to cultivate moral strength, virtue, and the individual pursuit of the reward of heaven in the context of highly organized religious communities. It was more about saving one's *own* soul from the dangers of wealth rather than a commitment to alleviate poverty or uplift the poorer classes. Nevertheless, monasteries, convents, churches, and lay-organized confraternities and new religious orders (Beguines) in the Middle Ages did provide some hospitality and compassionate care for the poor and sick of society to fulfill the seven corporeal works of mercy outlined in Matt 25:31–46,[24] while charity by the wealthy—including toward those who had

---

22. Basil preached a series of homilies on wealth. This one was based on Matt 19:16–22. Basil, *On Social Justice*, 43.

23. Chrysostom, *On Wealth and Poverty*, 49–50.

24. Lynn, *Christian Compassion*, 84–102.

vowed willingly to poverty—was viewed as a spiritual credit deposited in their spiritual accounts.[25]

By the time of the Renaissance and Reformation, however, many monasteries were far from the houses of holiness they claimed to be and that had once upon a time attracted widespread admiration and respect. As the Dutch humanist reformer Erasmus noted (if not exaggerated), the original quest for humility had been corrupted by boasting in self-righteousness.[26]

The perennial weakness of fallen human nature before the triple temptations of wealth, power, and fame—the fruits of self-love—reverberates in spiritual classics throughout the medieval, Renaissance, and Reformation periods. The medieval poet Dante encounters simoniacs, or clergy who greedily purchased church positions, in hell: "Gold and silver are the gods you adore! In what are you different from the idolator, save that he worships one, and you a score?"[27] In purgatory, envy is among the seven deadly sins for which souls in a state of grace willingly endure discipline and purgation before entering Paradise: "It is because you focus on the prize of worldly goods, which every sharing lessens that Envy pumps the bellows for your sighs. But if, in true love for the Highest Sphere, your longing were turned upward, then your hearts would never be consumed by such a fear; for the more there are who say 'ours'—not 'mine'—by that much is each richer, and the brighter within that cloister burns the Love Divine."[28] Hoarding of wealth is also maligned by the idealist communitarians of Thomas More's *Utopia*: "What shall I say of them that keep superfluous riches, to take delectation only in the beholding and not in the use or occupying thereof. . . . Or of them that be in a contrary vice, hiding the gold which they shall never occupy, nor peradventure never see more? . . . For what is it else when they hide it in the ground, taking it both from their own use and perchance from all other men's also?"[29] Lust for money is praised by Folly in Erasmus's powerful Renaissance satire: "Whenever you mix among the popes, princes, judges, magistrates, your friends, your enemies, the great, and the humble, you will discover that all disputes and other matters are resolved through the exchange of money; since the wise have no regard for money, here is all

---

25. Lindberg, *Beyond Charity*, 22–33, 66–67.
26. Erasmus, "Praise of Folly," 148–50.
27. Dante, *Inferno*, 156 (canto 19, lines 106–8).
28. Dante, *Purgatorio*, 147 (canto 15, lines 49–57).
29. More, "Utopia," 80.

the more reason to avoid them."[30] It was desire for honor, fame, and power that caused Christopher Marlowe's Doctor Faustus to abandon the study of Lutheran divinity for magic, selling his soul to the devil: "Of what a world of profit and delight, of power, of honor, of omnipotence, Is promised to the studious artisan! All things that move shall be at my command.... A sound magician is a mighty god. Here, Faustus, try they brains to gain a deity."[31]

The Era of Protestant Reform and Revival

The Protestant Reformers pointed to the materialistic ambition, corruption, and scheming violence at the highest levels of leadership in the late medieval Roman church as validation for their own religious cause.[32] Martin Luther had begun his own pursuit of divine acceptance through the medieval strategy of spiritual and material poverty as an Augustinian monk in 1505, but he soon cowered increasingly before the glare of a righteous God who demanded absolute, impossible perfection.[33] Standing up to centuries of developed tradition and the exalted claims of papal and episcopal authority, whose credibility was crumbling from tales of medieval corruption, Luther's revolutionary ideas based on the supreme authority of the biblical word and the satisfaction of heavenly merit in the righteousness of Christ alone would effectively lead to the elimination of the one-thousand-year-old institutions of monasticism in emerging Protestant lands. Although positive qualities of the monastic life and their cultural achievements were ignored or underemphasized by Protestant Reformers, the medieval piety of poverty was passé, and no longer was charity to the poor to be used as a stepping stone to achieve personal righteousness before God, nor was there any special merit with God to be found in choosing a life of beggary.

Luther has often been criticized for dividing the two kingdoms of the spiritual and temporal, for caring only about personal salvation, doctrinal issues, and ecclesiastical concerns, and less about programs of public policy or social reform.[34] His turning against German peasants in their militant revolutions for justice and his shameful hate speech towards the Jews later in life suggested that his theology might have little to contribute

30. Erasmus, "Praise of Folly," 161.
31. Marlowe, *Doctor Faustus*, 6 (act 1, scene 1).
32. Gregory, *Unintended Reformation*, 366–67.
33. Hendrix, *Martin Luther*, 27–40.
34. Lindberg, *Beyond Charity*, 161–63.

constructively—if not to obstruct—new thinking on social ethics. However, it was Luther's emphasis upon the authority of the word and salvation as "the foundation of life rather than the goal" that enabled the security of faith (and work and money) to be redirected away from self-interested religious transactions and decreasing of purgatorial pains toward the needs of the *living* neighbor more genuinely. For Luther, it was the reformation of the *root* (of doctrine and thus of true worship), not the fruit, that was of first and paramount importance for any possible hope of personal, and then societal, improvement in Christian obedience.[35]

Nevertheless, Luther did speak biblically into issues of moral legislation and civil government. As it relates to the closing of monasteries and religious houses, Luther determined that the evacuated populations would need provision and support from the church communities and the state to establish a new mode of living. Also, there remained the "legitimate poor"—those who were poor from circumstances outside their control, including old age, family loss, or handicap. For these, the churches—and increasingly the new Protestant governments—of the cities of the Reformation would take responsibility for administering a common fund or chest after the example of the early Christians to eliminate the need for begging (Acts 2:44–45 and 4:32–35; interestingly, these same passages had inspired the literal equality-in-simplicity model adopted by ancient monastic rules).[36]

As business, commerce, and trade flourished, and the urban middle class emerged as a potent social force in the European economy, it became requisite to address the Christian stewarding and distribution of expanding wealth rather than continuing to ennoble a medieval view of poverty. Along with other forms of economic corruption in monopolies, excessive luxury, wealth hoarding, and price gouging, Luther was critical of interest on loans (usury), recognizing this as one Levitical commandment to preserve based on the natural law of reason. Government regulation and laws were needed to deal with the greedy swindlers and loan evaders, as true Christians who exercise love-born-of-gospel-faith in all their fair trading are a rarity in any society.[37]

---

35. Lindberg, *Beyond Charity*, 95–127, 163–69.

36. Luther, "Obedience of a Common Chest" and "Fraternal Agreement on the Common Chest," in *Luther's Works*, 169–94. For the church orders of Lutheran cities, see also Lindberg, *Beyond Charity*, 129–45.

37. Luther, "On Trade and Usury," 246–50, 255–62; Lindberg, *Beyond Charity*, 112–14.

Although the Reformation movements pinned moral problems of society ultimately on doctrinal aberration and a chaining of the gospel in the medieval world, it did not take long for Protestant churches to become deformed by similar vices. As testified by Lutheran father of German Pietism, Philip Spener, 150 years after Luther posted the Ninety-Five Theses (1517), many German Lutheran clergy wielded a "worldly spirit" in their desire for promotion in wealth and reputation that contradicted the faith of the humble Christ they professed to know and defend.[38]

In the wake of the European Thirty Years' War (1618–48), German descendants of Luther's Reformation applied their Protestant faith to prophesying against impiety within their own churches, reformed states, and economic practices in a movement of Pietism under the leadership of men like Spener, Count Nicholas von Zinzendorf, and August Hermann Francke. Pietism may have been focused more on stoking the fires of personal spirituality and devotion to Christ through renewed focus on the word and the establishment of smaller lay prayer and Scripture groups, but it also contributed to the organization of welfare programs and philanthropic institutions devoted to empowerment of all believers as priests in Christ. Along with the establishment of the University of Halle, which became one of the leading missionary training schools for Protestants in Europe in the eighteenth century, Francke's widow and orphan homes provided education and spiritual formation of the young for future callings of worldly service.[39]

Inspired in part by the Pietists, a series of evangelical awakenings within Protestant denominations fueled movements of social reform in nineteenth-century Great Britain and North America. With optimism in the power of revival to prepare for the coming millennium, the nineteenth century witnessed the establishment of anti-slavery societies, temperance unions to curb the abuses of (or in some cases eliminate) alcohol use, religious education organizations, and domestic and foreign missionary bodies. Faith was applied to the spiritual fruits of social change in positive ways, not only through primarily inspiring individuals with a new moral conscience through evangelism but through secondary pressure on formal legislation to end evils on a social level as well.[40]

---

38. Spener, *Pia Desideria*, 45–46.

39. Brown, *Understanding Pietism*, 86–89, 100–102; Lynn, *Christian Compassion*, 124–25; Noll et al., *Turning Points*, 207–11.

40. Smith, *Revivalism and Social Reform*, 149–55, 161, 167, 176–77; Wolffe, *Expansion*

The Age of Industrialism

With the rise of industrial urbanization, the problem of the poor especially came to the forefront of the minds of many Christians with a compassionate social conscience, including such questions as discerning fair wages, which could not be merely answered by encouraging individual almsgiving. Mission houses were established in urban slums by Protestant women such as Methodist Phoebe Palmer to provide spiritual formation for needy souls, and eventually developed more coordinated material welfare and transition assistance to care for their needy *bodies* as well, which inspired the later work of organizations such as the YMCA. By the middle of the nineteenth century, several hundred such urban missions existed, often tied to denominational churches, but some joined together across denominational lines.[41] What Roman Catholics possessed in the legacy of female religious orders for charitable work, such as the Sisters of Mercy,[42] nineteenth-century Protestants developed in their own voluntary missionary organizations and para-church ministries (including the Salvation Army), many that began initially from evangelistic efforts to reach the new contexts of industrialized urban poverty. Yet there was a lack of universal agreement on the causes and solutions of poverty. Concerns were voiced even at the beginning of the industrial period, such as by the Scottish minister Thomas Chalmers, that the priority and power of evangelistic ministry would be overshadowed by charitable work and that well-intentioned charity could be exploited to accentuate dependency.[43]

In Victorian Britain, it was Quaker minister Elizabeth "Betsy" Fry who was the female face of philanthropy in her quest to bring mercy and compassion for lost souls into reform of the English prison system. After her visit to the notorious Newgate prison, where the appalling overcrowded horrors of filth, half-nakedness, and hunger met her religious spirit, she set about with her Ladies Association to introduce "occupation, instruction, religion, and cleanliness" into the prison to help in the rehabilitation of thieves and prostitute women (and their children).[44] She was also moved

---

of *Evangelicalism*, 178–83; Lynn, *Christian Compassion*, 139–40.

41. Smith, *Revivalism and Social Reform*, 170–75.

42. Lynn, *Christian Compassion*, 129–30, 148–49.

43. Wolffe, *Expansion of Evangelicalism*, 183–86, 192; Lynn, *Christian Compassion*, 141, 144.

44. Wilberforce even made a visit and praised the work. Rose, *Elizabeth Fry*, 94–95.

by the callous treatment of the mentally insane in prisons and spoke out on behalf of male and female prisoners against the liberal use of the death penalty for petty crimes. Although not a feminist or suffragette like Lucretia Mott or Elizabeth Cady Stanton in the United States, Fry utilized her ascending public notoriety to advocate for more centralized government reform of prisons throughout England.

In the United States, Walter Rauschenbusch, pastor of a German Baptist church in the slums of Hell's Kitchen, New York, in the 1880s and 90s, discovered that the revivalist evangelical message of individual salvation and the promise of heaven was not effectively engaging this-worldly problems facing the poor immigrant working class and the daily maltreatment families endured in the new industrial wilderness driven by competitive greed. Rauschenbusch became a leading spokesman of what became known as the "Social Gospel," directing much of his prophetic calls for conversion and reform to the wealthy and powerful: "The primary means to accomplish this change was not through political activism, but through moral suasion, where the teachings of Christ would appeal to the consciences of the powerful to change social structures."[45] Nevertheless, he also advocated for a soft, democratic movement toward socialism and increased government regulation to curb some of the laissez-faire excesses of early twentieth-century capitalism in hopes of leading America toward a closer approximation of the kingdom of God on earth in social solidarity. Rauschenbusch and the "Social Gospel" are often tied negatively to a liberal Protestant program that diminished theological orthodoxy and ascribed kingdom building to social-economic-political efforts, but Rauschenbusch's background in the German Pietist and American Protestant post-millennial revivalist heritage influenced his retention of an evangelical understanding of the essential importance of individual, spiritual conversion.[46] Wealth alone was not enough to make individuals whole and happy, but the deprivation of sufficient wealth to the point of poor health and hunger was also a basic obstruction toward human dignity and flourishing. What Rauschenbusch did contribute, considering the problems of poverty and exploitation in urban industrial life, was a focus on the ethical, this-worldly implications of conversion and Christian life for both individuals and social institutions: "No man shares his life with God whose religion does not flow out, naturally

---

45. Evans, *Kingdom Is Always but Coming*, xx–xxi.

46. Rauschenbusch translated into German the Gospel hymns of Ira Sankey, D. L. Moody's evangelism partner. Evans, *Kingdom Is Always but Coming*, xxix.

and without effort, into all relations of his life and reconstructs everything that it touches. Whoever uncouples the religious and the social life has not understood Jesus."[47] This was a time in the US where a large proportion of the population still professed to be Christian, and where Rauschenbusch could sound his appeal based on the Old Testament prophets of justice and the fundamental virtue of love inculcated by Jesus and exemplified by the primitive Christian community.[48] Although Rauschenbusch was more conservative regarding women's primarily domestic responsibilities, and he had less to say about the unequal plight of African Americans, Rauschenbusch's application of Christianity to social reconstruction inspired the likes of later civil rights leaders such as the black Baptist preacher Martin Luther King Jr.

Racial Justice

There are times in Christianity's history when, in friendship to Christ, many have had to—like Jesus—stand up to challenge those of their common faith and nation to call out the unrighteousness and injustice of their supposedly Christianized societies.[49] It cannot be denied that Christians in history have sadly *protected* their power and privilege in oppressive systems and allowed their love of God expressed in *eros* and *storge* to act like an opiate promising heaven while lacking more serious zeal for righting the wrongs of *this* world.[50] Although not true of all Christianity, Nussbaum aptly characterizes the legacy of an Augustinian emphasis on spiritual longing or desire for God and heaven that softens the urgencies of confronting evil in history: "The aim of slipping off into beatitude distracts moral attention from the

---

47. Rauschenbusch, *Christianity and the Social Crisis*, 42. In 1947, Carl F. H. Henry, a theologically conservative neo-evangelical, indicted American Protestant Fundamentalists for disengaging their individualistic faith from broader, this-worldly social concerns. Henry, *Uneasy Conscience of Modern Fundamentalism*.

48. Rauschenbusch, *Christianity and the Social Crisis*, 39–116. The official and magisterial Roman Catholic response to the problems of industrial society were promulgated first with the encyclical *Rerum Novarum* issued by Pope Leo XIII in 1892. See *Compendium*, 39–47 and 114–61.

49. "If ever the book which I am not going to write is written it must be the full confession by Christendom of Christendom's specific contribution to the sum of human cruelty and treachery. . . . We have shouted the name of Christ and enacted the service of Moloch." Lewis, *Four Loves*, 30.

50. Packer and Howard, *Christianity*, 19; Niebuhr, *Beyond Tragedy*, 233–34.

Philia

goal of making this world a good world, and encourages a focus on one's own moral safety that does not bode well for earthly justice."[51]

Yet there are examples to the contrary in the history of the faith. William Wilberforce, a member of the British House of Commons, combined an experience of Protestant evangelical awakening with a burden to fight this-worldly social evils. In 1785–86, he experienced a new-birth conversion from a life of gambling, partying, and culturally respectable religious morality, contemplated leaving politics for pastoral ministry, but was persuaded to remain in Parliament and persevere in the goal of seeing the African slave trade—and slavery—abolished throughout the British Empire (which occurred without civil war and fifty years before emancipation was declared in the United States).[52] Just days before he died John Wesley, the Methodist Reformer of Anglicanism, wrote to Wilberforce to encourage his efforts. Wesley preached a higher sanctification of the fruit of faith in active love, especially in moderate living, stewardship, and philanthropic liberality toward others in need.[53] Wilberforce also devoted himself to forming religious societies devoted to uplifting the poor and pressed for legislation in reforming public morality, or the "Reformation of Manners."[54]

In nations that professed to be populated by Christians, that an institution such as the enslavement of Africans against their will ever existed to the degree that it did at all—and justified by twisting the Bible to support theories of ethnic superiority—is an unsightly paradox of moral hypocrisy that defied loving God in friendship with Jesus and arguably demonstrated a complacent *storge* unaccompanied by *philia*. In the words of ex-slave Frederick Douglass, "I love the pure, peaceable, and impartial Christianity of Christ: I therefore hate the corrupt, slaveholding, women-whipping, cradle-plundering, partial and hypocritical Christianity of this land."[55] As early as the late 1700s, evangelical Anglican-Methodist clergy like John Wesley

---

51. "Ascent has carried the lover too far beyond the realm of worldly need, suffering, and injustice for her to be quick to fight for the neighbor's right, or to assuage the neighbor's pain . . . will take her away from morality itself." Nussbaum, *Upheavals of Thought*, 553, 556.

52. Tomkins, *William Wilberforce*; Wolffe, *Expansion of Evangelicalism*, 199–201.

53. Lynn, *Christian Compassion*, 135.

54. Tomkins, *William Wilberforce*, 54–55; Wilberforce also promoted reforms in hospital care, prison life, and industrial factories. Rosell, "Foreword," ix.

55. Douglass, "Appendix," in *Narrative*, 100. Timothy Smith aptly entitles one of his chapters "Christian Liberty and Human Bondage: The Paradox of Slavery," in *Revivalism and Social Reform*, 178–203.

spoke out against the evils of slavery, but it was Quakers on both sides of the Atlantic that formed the first formal organized committees to politically advocate for its abolition. While the slave system (though not racism) in New England states began to die away in the early 1800s, it remained entrenched in the Southern cotton-producing regions. Northern evangelical abolitionists varied in their approaches to ending slavery—immediate vs. gradual and the work of government vs. the fires of revival (Charles Finny)—and many carefully weighed a personal aversion toward southern slavery with concerns that moral pressure from revivalists would open a geographical fissure within their denominations and their united mission of evangelistic mission (Presbyterians divided in 1837–78; Methodists in 1843; and Baptists in 1845). Controversies over slavery and admission of new states and the occurrence of Nat Turner's slave revolt bled into heightened polarized Scripture polemics, denominational division, and Civil War.[56] While in a few instances, Christianity itself was attacked as a bedfellow to oppression of blacks and women, and though pro-slavery advocates in (mostly) the South viewed protection of slaveholding as a conservative defense of biblical interpretation, Scripture and the ethics of Christianity also formed the case for abolitionism and eventually the movement toward equality and integration.

Even after Emancipation in 1863 and the passing of the Thirteenth, Fourteenth, and Fifteenth Amendments, blacks were still not viewed equally in the North or South, and the rights blacks had gained in the era of Southern Reconstruction after the war were stripped from them by the reduction of the national powers of federal government and the retaliation of the majority of embittered Southern whites who enacted racist Jim Crow laws, suppressive policies of segregation, and vigilante violence in thousands of lynchings. Even Northern evangelical revivalist leaders after the Civil War turned their energies to heavenly salvation and personal conversion rather than political action.[57]

The black churches of the South, having been liberated to form their own separate congregations and denominations not controlled or dominated by whites, were the religious as well as the social and political culture of African Americans throughout the 1800s and early 1900s as they

---

56. Wolffe, *Expansion of Evangelicalism*, 208–11; Smith, *Revivalism and Social Reform*, 180–203; Noll, *Civil War*; Kidd, *America's Religious History*, 125–37.

57. Raboteau, *Canaan Land*, 71–72; Noll, *God and Race*, 70–80; Kidd, *America's Religious History*, 230–31.

were excluded by whites from public life.[58] Ethicist Reinhold Niebuhr in 1932 considered that it would take a grassroots movement, like Gandhi's in India for independence from the colonial British raj, and spearheaded by blacks themselves to awaken the moral conscience of white populations and apply nonviolent pressure on political policies for equality.[59] It was in the black churches, with a religious impulse significantly inspired by God-given human dignity, the love of Christ, and a hope for deliverance held out to the oppressed in Scripture, that the agitation for civil rights began in the 1930s and 1940s. Pastors like Martin Luther King Jr. and Howard Thurman became leaders and spokespersons for the black community supported by grassroots campaigns led by black women. The Christianity that many African Americans had first learned from their oppressors had become internalized as their own hope of liberation and flourishing that inspired coordinated nonviolent movements for equality, justice, and full integration into society—a mutual sharing together in the world of "a common humanity."[60]

Personal observations of the race divide by German Lutheran pastor Dietrich Bonhoeffer in his visits to Harlem, New York City, in 1930–31 left an indelible impact on his own theology of suffering resistance to Nazi racist ideology when he returned to his homeland and was later martyred in Flossenbürg concentration camp in 1945. Where many of his Lutheran pastoral colleagues supported the government or remained quiet, Bonhoeffer stood in open solidarity with the Jewish population increasingly marginalized under Hitler's government and the alignment of German Christians with promises of nationalist prosperity.[61] As Bonhoeffer stated in his *Letters and Papers from Prison*, "The church must share in the secular problems of

---

58. Bebbington, *Dominance of Evangelicalism*, 231–32.

59. Niebuhr, *Moral Man*, 252–54. Gandhi's influence on Civil Rights leaders is well documented. Howard Thurman and Martin Luther King Jr. were influenced by Mahatma Gandhi's teachings on the moral high ground of nonviolent resistance in British-ruled India. Raboteau, *Canaan Land*, 105–13; Noll, *God and Race*, 109, 111. Gandhi was influenced by Leo Tolstoy's identification with the peasant class in pre-revolutionary, aristocratic Russia. Gandhi first developed his nonviolent program while residing in South Africa, including establishment of "Tolstoyan farms," on behalf of fellow Indians living in South Africa. Fischer, *Gandhi*, 39–42.

60. Thurman, *Jesus and the Disinherited*, 88–90; King, "Letter from a Birmingham Jail," 199–201; also Roberts, *Black Religion*, 31–60.

61. Williams, "Dietrich Bonhoeffer," 60–64. Bonhoeffer had planned to make his own visit to Gandhi, but it never transpired.

ordinary human life, not dominating, but helping and serving. It must tell people of every calling what it means to live in Christ, to exist for others."[62]

It was largely the Christian spirit that fueled the push for civil disobedience and calls for international economic sanctions to end the racist system of apartheid in South Africa in the 1970s to 1990s, led by Anglican Bishop Desmond Tutu. Although often linked to Marxist militant fronts such as the Soviet-aided African National Congress (ANC), Tutu favored diplomatic efforts between the white-controlled government and disinherited black South Africans and more biblically permissible, peaceful strategies of active resistance through public demonstrations against policies of the State supported by the majority-racist Dutch Reformed Church.[63] Following South Africa's first democratically free election of ex-prisoner Nelson Mandela as President of the new republic in 1994, Mandela and Tutu spearheaded the Truth and Reconciliation Commission as a way of holding Afrikaner white supremacists responsible to issue public repentance and provide reparation (restorative justice) for the evils of the apartheid system that oppressed the dignity and flourishing of black south Africans, yet without exacting vengeful retaliation. The successful future of the new South Africa for Tutu and others lay not in aggravating estrangement by returning hatred for hatred but in mutual restoration and healed relationships between oppressor and victim through a synthesis of traditional African *ubuntu*, biblical repentance, and the healing power of Christian forgiveness.[64]

The Age of Reason, Modern Philosophy, and the Moral Jesus

Loving God in friendship with Christ, however, must not become severed from the root of abiding in him (John 15:5), a love formed and expressed through the habits of liturgical worship (*storge*) and the desire for a personal knowledge and experience of union with God (*eros*). Whereas for Luther it was a desire for the freedom of biblical Christian faith from bondage to sixteenth-century Roman Catholicism, beginning with René Descartes it was doubt in the whole collected, handed-down disposition of religious thought that led him to assume nothing for granted accept his rational,

---

62. Bonhoeffer, *Letters and Papers*, 369–70.
63. Allen, *Rabble-Rouser for Peace*, 283–92.
64. Allen, *Rabble-Rouser for Peace*, 342, 346–47; Tutu, *No Future without Forgiveness*.

thinking self ("I think, therefore I am").[65] German Enlightenment philosopher Immanuel Kant blasted uncritical conformity to the religious and political worldview coming from outside of himself, declaring on behalf of autonomous individual reason: "*Sapere Aude!*" ("Have courage to use your own understanding!")[66] It was the conventions of human society that Jean-Jacques Rousseau blamed for the inevitable competition and corruption of individuals who are naturally innocent.[67] A revolt against handed-down dispositions and traditions, including church liturgies and biblical interpretation, inspired successive movements to liberate the self (and in turn humanity) from such needless restraints in a new modern age of self-made individuals, societies, and nations.[68]

Moral philosophers of the eighteenth-century Enlightenment believed that God-given natural human reason was sufficient to guide ethical behavior, and a few atheists even provocatively asserted that belief in a God was not necessary—but even a hindrance—to a life of moral virtue. As stated by atheist d'Holbach: "To learn the true principles of morality, men have no need of theology, of revelation, or gods. They have need only of reason. . . . To found morality upon a God, whom everyone paints to himself differently, composes in his own way, and arranges according to his own temperament and interest, is evidently to found morality upon the caprice and imagination of men."[69] The new philosophical impulse among elite intellectuals in France, Great Britain, and North America demystified religion in the interests of human reason and science as authorities and in the wake of wars that involved religious (liturgical and theological) divisions. Moral virtue and human flourishing defined the pure religion of the Enlightenment, and for French thinkers like Voltaire and Jean-Jacques Rousseau and Germany's Immanuel Kant this included bias against organized church worship and the practicing of pious spiritual disciplines of contemplative prayer and study of the Bible.[70]

65. Descartes, "I Think, Therefore," 184.

66. Kant, "Answer to the Question," 41.

67. Rousseau, "Second Discourse."

68. See Maritain, *Three Reformers*; Taylor, *Sources of the Self*, 111–210; Trueman, *Rise and Triumph*. The new individualism fit the culture of American opportunism. Bellah et al., *Habits of the Heart*, 82–83.

69. d'Holbach, "No Need of Theology," 144, 146.

70. Taylor, *Secular Age*, 221–24. In Voltaire's *Candide*, the main character stumbles upon the lost utopian city of El Dorado, where he experiences a unified, monotheistic religion without division and priesthood. Voltaire, *Candide*, 70–71.

Rousseau believed that a religious impulse was necessary for the good of the state, but not in the form of any of the historical churches. His was a purely "civil religion," akin to deism, limited "to the purely internal worship of the supreme God and to the eternal duties of morality . . . the pure and simple religion of the Gospel, the true theism." Rousseau personally rejected Christian *storge* and defined the spirit of social religion as responsible citizenship, commitment to nationalism, and a morality of brotherhood in the social contract. On the one hand, the state establishment of one form of religion by natural necessity leads to division and sundering of the state. On the other hand, foreshadowing by a century the thought of Marx—who moved beyond deism to atheism—Rousseau considered the historical Christianity of Jesus as weakening the social contract by encouraging focus on heaven and an indifferent passivity toward social circumstances, including national defense.[71]

The Enlightenment, from within the midst of quarreling denominational confessions and states, put the spotlight on religion as a moral impulse that benefits social life in *this* world. The New Testament teaches that faith without works is indeed dead (Jas 2:26), and true religion that "God our Father accepts" involves care for the orphan and widow (Jas 1:27). Loving God merely or in excess through liturgical habits (*storge*), as well as in personal, contemplative desire (*eros*), but without active moral friendship to Christ (*philia*) can result in a reduced and deficient Christianity that is complacent, irresponsible, or disinterested in engaging the problems of this world and age.

Yet, in excessive reaction, Enlightenment moralism also disconnected the supernatural energy of virtue formed and expressed in liturgy (*storge*) and the spiritual experiences of personal soul-union with God (*eros*). The result was almost exclusive focus on the bettering of this world and by means of a confidence in the strength and potential of autonomous human reason, science, and moral agency.[72] While philanthropy may have still been considered a social virtue by the new free thinkers, and movement toward pan-Europeanism and international peace was the reasoned ideal, the modern age witnessed the classical and medieval spirit of nationalism and militant heroism that contributed to the sobering horrors of nineteenth

---

71. Rousseau, "Social Contract," 250–53.

72. Ward depicts this as the modern clash between the Baconian spirit of science in mastery of nature and the Augustinian focus on waiting for God, the future, and heavenly life. Ward, *Robert Elsmere*, 160.

and twentieth-century violence.[73] H. Richard Niebuhr acknowledged that movements in historical Christianity of "withdrawal and renunciation" should flow into "an equally necessary movement of responsible engagement in cultural tasks," but he considered the former necessary to keep Christianity from becoming simply another instrument of some social or political mission other than that of the Lord's: "The church becomes an instrument of state, unable to point men to their transpolitical identity and their suprapolitical loyalty . . . one more group of power-hungry or security-seeking men."[74] His brother Reinhold similarly spoke of how believing in "one story" under "one divine sovereignty" in biblical Christian faith prevents humanity from deifying the meaning of history in the achievements of "ages and cultures, civilizations and philosophies" and from equating that meaning with "their cause or the completion of their particular project."[75]

As Lewis stated in *The Four Loves* regarding each human love, they become demons precisely when they become gods. In Enlightenment thought, "the practice of virtue was the only form of cult worthy of God."[76] However, when ethics were severed from life in Christ, rather than being complementary to *storge* and *eros*, as was the vision of Pietism and evangelical revivalism in the eighteenth century, it drifted into a naïve and destructive optimism in human knowledge and moral effort, both individual and collective, for making ideal states and ultimately one ideal world.[77] As Richard Foster states in his discussion of the "social justice" stream of historical Christianity, "the Church has deeper reasons for its existence and ministry,

---

73. Derek Wilson, "Past Tense and Future Conditional," 191–92, 198–99; Taylor, *Secular Age*, 225, 233–34, 245, 263. See also chapter 5 in this book, "Fractured Loves and the Secular Age."

74. This is in context of his analysis of "Christ against Culture" movements, which he views as offering one necessary, though all by itself inadequate, answer to the Christ and culture problem. Niebuhr, *Christ and Culture*, 65–68. Niebuhr, in referencing the perspective of F. D. Maurice, critiques a Christianity of "external rites" that is socially unconcerned as well as the dangers of science-based moralism divorced from theological foundations of human personality. Niebuhr, *Christ and Culture*, 222.

75. Niebuhr, *Faith and History*, 119.

76. Taylor, *Secular Age*, 222.

77. Niebuhr, "Assurance of Grace," in Brown, *Essential Reinhold Niebuhr*, 71. "The final victory over man's disorder is God's and not ours, but we do have a responsibility for proximate victories." Niebuhr, "Christian Witness," in Brown, *Essential Reinhold Niebuhr*, 100; Niebuhr, *Faith and History*, 206.

reasons that are fundamentally spiritual in nature. For Christians social justice concerns must always be rooted in profound spiritual realities."[78]

Must acknowledging human weakness require belief in a historical fall? Is it necessary that Jesus' death on a cross be understood as a substitutionary atonement for people to be morally transformed? Are the historic, liturgical creeds of Christian orthodoxy necessary facts of history or can modern society remove a universal moral-ethical (humanitarian) kernel from the husk of Christian supernatural myth, as modern thinkers like Thomas Jefferson, Friedrich Strauss, Leo Tolstoy, and Adolf von Harnack attempted?[79] This was the provocative topic of the sermon preached by Mr. Grey in *Robert Elsmere*: Is the spiritual resurrection of Christ in Christians to a new moral life *dependent* upon "alleged historical events"? Is Christianity the "spiritual history of the individual and the world" and not "the envelope of miracle to which hitherto mankind has attributed so much importance"?[80]

Deists of the seventeenth- and eighteenth-century Enlightenment believed they could adopt the morality of Jesus excised of his eternal and supernatural life and extricate it from the communal context of traditional worship (*storge*). The life of Jesus, then, was an example for individual or collective social ethics (*philia*), but he did not now live in heaven as the object of prayer and worship (*eros*), the divine *logos* of a new creation inaugurated through the actual historical events of his miraculous life, substitutionary death, bodily resurrection, ascension to heaven, and sending of the person of the Holy Spirit to indwell believers.[81]

Moral law divorced from liturgical worship and prayerful communion with God was, although exemplified in the man Jesus, considered adequately discoverable by unaided human reason and attainable through unaided human willpower. Not only were moral theorists themselves divided (natural law, utilitarian, Kantian/deontological, nihilist, etc.),[82] but moral reasoning also became exploited by the authority of rising nationalist, militarist, and racist ideologies in the twentieth century.[83] Morality

---

78. Foster, *Streams of Living Water*, 179.

79. E.g., Strauss, *Life of Jesus*; Tolstoy, "What Is Religion," 94–96; Tolstoy, "Religion and Morality"; Harnack, *What Is Christianity?*

80. Ward, *Robert Elsmere*, 81, 82.

81. Taylor, *Secular Age*, 291.

82. See Boyd and Thorsen, *Christian Ethics*.

83. E.g., Kater, *Hitler Youth*, 8.

was ultimately defined by nationalist goals of the state—even when that state justified oppression toward its own or against other nations to serve the new cause of creating a new god from humanity and a new heaven on earth through the new religion of science and the politics of revolution or empire.[84] The church in the interest of self-preservation was forced with the choice to align itself with and prop up the new regimes or be pushed out of the way: "The history of the Christian Church is replete with the embarrassing submissions of prophets and priests to the pride and arrogance of nations and rulers."[85] Rejection of this association of Christianity with a morality determined by national patriotism was what eventually got Dietrich Bonhoeffer hung in Nazi Germany in 1945 two years after his fellow prisoner at Tegel in Berlin, the conscientious Austrian farmer and Roman Catholic Franz Jägerstätter, was beheaded.[86] In El Salvador in 1980, Archbishop Romero was assassinated while performing Mass as a revolutionary because of his vocal solidarity with the poorer classes in confrontation with the government: "The much-desired, long-sought-after goal of harmony between the church and the powers of this world—the state, the armed forces, economic powers, political powers—simply did not figure among Archbishop Romero's goals."[87]

G. K. Chesterton once asked why we must have and believe Christian doctrines to be moral agents. His answer was that Christianity gives an "intellectual justification for my intuitions."[88] Separating meaning from myth (as if ahistorical) ultimately ended for many in challenging or denying the *meaning* and the myth altogether. Dismissing the historical fact of the Fall made it easier to abandon the *meaning* of the Fall: that death and self-destruction results from lusting after the pride of knowledge, seeking freedom and independence from the obedience and worship of God, and ignoring the inescapable limits of our creatureliness and need for the help

---

84. On Hegel, Nietzsche, the "growing omnipotence of the State," and dehumanization, see Camus, *Rebel*, 141–42, 177–85, 192–96, 233–35. See also Orwell, *1984*.

85. Niebuhr, *Beyond Tragedy*, 84–87.

86. Jägerstätter, *Letters and Writings*. After Austria was occupied by the Reich beginning in 1938, Jägerstätter was beheaded in 1943 for refusing the oath of allegiance to Hitler and for disavowing military service in the Austrian army because he firmly believed Hitler's aggressive invasion of other countries was unjust.

87. Archbishop Romero, like Martin Luther King Jr., never advocated popular movements of violence (Communist) when speaking out for the liberation of the oppressed. Sobrino, *Archbishop Romero*, 10, 27; Romero, *Violence of Love*.

88. Chesterton, *Orthodoxy*, 149–50.

of his grace.[89] This does not mean that Christians are innocent of great evils, or that a secular humanist who does not believe in original sin is incapable of works of charity. In fact, a moral nihilist would argue that it takes greater heroism and courage to do good in the face of a godless, meaningless, and ultimately hopeless universe of absurdity. However, there are *sources* of morality in Christianity's historical events and doctrines that divinely empower mankind's efforts at benevolence, preserve the humility needed to *sustain* selfless, unconditional love, as well as restrain self-confident moral idealism and human philanthropy from becoming jaded misanthropy or self-righteous paternalism.[90] Prime Minister of Great Britain William Gladstone, in criticizing the liberal perspective of Ward's *Robert Elsmere* in 1888, noted its aim to

> expel the preternatural element of Christianity, to destroy its dogmatic structure, yet to keep intact the moral and spiritual results. . . . Such sanguine hopefulness is a Christian brotherhood, but with a Christianity emptied of that which Christians believe to be the soul and springhead of its life. . . . A living and a Divine Person, to whom they are to be united by a vital incorporation. It is the reunion to God of a nature severed from God by sin, and the process is one, not of teaching lessons, but of imparting a new life, with its ordained equipment of gifts and powers.[91]

The reduction of God's activity among Enlightenment Deists to the creation of nature and natural law was followed by the emptying of heaven and the identification of nature and the process of history *with* an impersonal deity among some nineteenth-century pantheistic Romantics—a paganized *eros* that sought for emotional connection with the mystery of self-consciousness, mind, and beauty. Then, the rise of atheistic materialism and nihilism—as in Friedrich Nietzsche—emptied the heavens *and the* earth of the mystery of the divine altogether, to be replaced with the deification of humanity free to create its own future alone by a capricious will to power in the face of death and ultimate meaninglessness.[92] Instead of nature reflecting and bearing the image of the creator, God was viewed as simply the discarded image and reflection (or creation) *of* nature. As the Queen of the dark Underland in Lewis's book *The Silver Chair* tried to lull

---

89. Taylor, *Secular Age*, 222.
90. Taylor, *Secular Age*, 695–99, 702, 709.
91. "Appendix D—Gladstone's Response," in Ward, *Robert Elsmere*, 679.
92. Camus, *Rebel*, 65–82, 100–103.

Philia

Jill, Puddleglum, Scrubb, and Prince Rilian, "Come, all of you. Put away these childish tricks. I have work for you all in the real world. There is no Narnia, *no Overworld*, no sky, no sun, no Aslan" (my italics).[93]

Lewis observed that what Hinduism separates from the Brahmin *ashram* and the Hindu temple, Christianity integrates; while it brings us into conformity with "an enlightened universalist ethic" it continues to invite us to participate in local, liturgical celebrations of worship: "a Mystery, to drink the blood of the Lord."[94] The Christian love of God cannot be reduced to living a good, noble, moral life for others through individual acts of charity or collective efforts at social change, even following the likeness of Jesus. This exclusive moralist focus was taken to excess in the optimism of modern Deism. In the context of European religious division and war over biblical doctrines and church ceremonies, Deists—much like the later "death of God" and secular theologies of the 1960s—naïvely assumed they could successfully unplug a rationalized human morality from what they perceived as primitive spiritual superstitions, which were really Christian beliefs in the necessary help of the transcendent, supernatural grace and power of God mediated through the truth of Scripture, the worship liturgy of the church, and personal, spiritual prayer. Western moral thought, loosened from the structures of revealed religion, was thereby subjected to the pretentious whims of spiritually unaided human reason and became vulnerable to the new gods of the state.[95] In the mind of the Danish philosopher Søren Kierkegaard, this is to limit the *telos* of human morality to only that which serves this world, and particularly its utilitarian purpose for the state, while Christian faith calls for a relationship to God of each individual lived before him as absolute that—if required—"suspends" the universal and the ethical (illustrated in Abraham's test of suffering to offer up Isaac

---

93. Lewis, *Silver Chair*, 180. "For their sciences are not concerned at all with the general relations of this country to anything that may lie East of it or West of it. . . . They have already decided that the fairest things of all—that is the Landlord, and if you like, the mountains and the Island—are a mere copy of this country." Lewis, *Pilgrim's Regress*, 61.

94. Lewis, "Christian Apologetics," in *God in the Dock*, 102–3. Lewis does describe a natural law and practical moral reason of benevolence found in many ancient philosophies and religions, what he calls the *Tao* in his *Abolition of Man*, in *Signature Classics*, 731–38. However, the uniqueness of Christ and Christianity is emphasized elsewhere. See his discussion of social morality and faith in *Mere Christianity*, in *Signature Classics*, 74–77, 121–22.

95. For all their criticism of traditional church religion, Voltaire and Thomas Jefferson believed that it served a provisional purpose for the masses unenlightened by moral reason. Taylor, *Secular Age*, 240.

in contradiction to what was "ethical" and defined by its "outcome"): "In his action he overstepped the ethical altogether, and had a higher *telos* outside it, in relation to which he suspended it. . . . It is not to save a nation, not to uphold the idea of the State, that Abraham did it, not to appease angry gods."[96] *Philia* with Christ curbs the validity of earthly citizenship and social responsibility from falling into excessive and uncritical devotion to the new god of the nation, culture, or society (Phil 3:20–21). The active moral life is essential to loving God but *philia* with Christ is needfully anchored to, empowered, and restrained by loving God through the church's liturgical worship and personal desire for union with God through prayer, contemplation, and meditation on Scripture.

---

96. Kierkegaard, *Fear and Trembling*, 88, 90–98. This is the kind of turn from the security of the universal (understood as moral duty to the State) to the isolation of the particular that imbibed the hidden life of Franz Jägerstätter in his refusal to fight for the Reich after the German annexation of Austria. See Jägerstätter, *Letters and Writings*.

3

Eros

Loving God in Desire for Personal Union

LEWIS ASSOCIATES *EROS* AMONG the four loves with the strong emotion of "being in love," arguably the one that dominates in our present romanticized and hyper-sexualized age. For Lewis, however, *eros* is more than bodily sexual desire, which he differentiates as "Venus." It is a "delighted preoccupation" with and desire for one particular person in "totality." It arises as an Appreciation-love that then develops into enamored desire for possession, as if to be united was a fulfillment of a predetermined plan. It is a desire for total union of body and soul, "to obliterate the distinction from giving and receiving."[1]

More powerful than even *storge* or *philia* the impulse of *eros* pledges absolute self-denial, willing to sacrifice any loss to life, health, or honor for the sake of the beloved. *Eros* would rather suffer than try and be happy apart: "Oh, happy dagger, this is thy sheath; there rust, and let me die," says Juliet before killing herself upon waking and discovering Romeo lying as if dead beside her.[2] *Eros* possesses "grandeur and terror," becoming god-like even as it becomes demon-like. Denying or renouncing the compulsion of *eros* seems tantamount to disobeying a sacred authority or to committing apostasy against an undeniable truth: "His total commitment, his reckless disregard of happiness, his transcendence of self-regard, sound like a

---

1. Lewis, *Four Loves*, 91–97.
2. Shakespeare, *Romeo and Juliet*, 1091 (act 5, scene 3).

message from the eternal world." Yet in that commanding voice, *eros* "may urge to evil as well as to good." It may bring together two that are in fact unsuitable, and it may break asunder promises and duties of an existing union. Its sacrificing of reason or ruining of conscience will even seem a quasi-religious duty whose suffering must be endured: "*Eros*, honoured without reservation and obeyed unconditionally, becomes a demon."[3] Because of its impulsive power to overcome reasonable resistance, *eros* is also the most dangerous and the most prone to become an idol, deaf to reason, and given to jealousy, possessiveness, and hate. Remember the uncharacteristic mental and emotional breakdown of Natasha Rostov after her plans to elope with Anatole Kurigan were obstructed by family and friends in Tolstoy's *War and Peace*.

In the *Symposium*, Plato defines *eros* as a desire to have what one does not yet have, a Will-to-Possess: "Man loves and desires only that which he wants and has not got, for who in the world would desire what he already has?" As in the *Phaedrus*, Plato describes the highest form of *eros* as the desire for union, not with a human person, but with the realm of pure ideas.[4] Although Lewis focuses most of his discussion of *eros* on human love, he does agree with Plato in *The Four Loves* and other writings that the desire that moves people should even more be true of desire for God, and secondarily the wellbeing of humanity as well. In this way, human *eros* images, even as "a preparation," the absolute devotion owed to God first.[5] That longings and desires, especially in human loves, are not *fulfilled* in or by nature points to their ultimate fulfillment beyond nature in God: "From the portraits to the Original, from the rivulets to the Fountain, from the creatures He made lovable to Love Himself."[6] Petersen describes this "Transcendent Desire" as a "Christianized Platonic *eros*" in Lewis.[7]

Lofty are the vows and promises that *eros* makes, but Lewis says these cannot be fulfilled by *eros* alone: "*Eros* is driven to perform what *Eros* himself cannot perform.... We must do the works of *Eros* when *Eros* is not present. This all good lovers know. [*Eros*] needs help." It is the most "mortal" of loves even though it is the one that most boasts its "permanency." How many marriages have fallen apart by those who have "idolised *Eros*"

---

3. Lewis, *Four Loves*, 107–13.
4. Plato, *Symposium*, in Cohen et al., *Readings*, 260–61.
5. Lewis, *Four Loves*, 110–11, 114; Leiva-Merikakis, *Love's Sacred Order*, 109–12.
6. Lewis, *Four Loves*, 139; *Pilgrim's Regress*, 212.
7. Peterson, *C. S. Lewis*, 32–46.

and who have chased after new experiences as if to find the next real thing?[8] Screwtape's counsel to Wormwood in Lewis's *Screwtape Letters* is to exploit the disappointment in the diminishing of enthusiasm and excitement that is experienced after a while by new Christian converts, much like what happens often after the first year or two between newlyweds.[9]

Eros: Desiring Spiritual Union with God

The burning bush, the still small voice, the Mount of Transfiguration, Paul on the road to Damascus, the apocalyptic visions of John the apostle; Scripture describes events of extraordinary encounters with God, a unique breaking through of the invisible dimension of heaven into history. These occurrences were rarer than they might appear in the biblical record, and while modern thought has tried to relegate most, if not all, to ahistorical myths, there remains a modern hunger to experience enchantment and mystery that takes us out of ourselves, even the natural world itself, into something more—an infinite reality that is deeply connected to our human experience and yet transcends and gives it meaning. G. K. Chesterton describes how, as an adult, nursery rhymes and fairy tales still possessed a more truthful view of the natural world for him, invoking a spiritual awe that had become lost in the impersonal order of modern scientific materialism: "Perhaps we all like astonishing tales because they touch the nerve of the ancient instinct of astonishment."[10] Lewis and his friend J. R. R. Tolkien both tapped into this natural hunger to be enchanted in their imaginative and immensely popular fantasy epics unsurpassable by anything Netflix can produce.

While creation points to the glory of God, wherein are seen his attributes of power, goodness, and beauty (Ps 91), there is also a longing to know the God who stands behind the world, so to speak. For Lewis, the reality of humanity is that it cannot ever truly be satisfied by God's gifts in creation. The real created hunger and desire is through them for the experience of God himself. The psalmist describes this as a panting of the soul (42:1 or 73:25), and Eccl 3:11 refers to the heart's desire and orientation toward infinity. The fifth-century bishop Augustine, after a journey of earthly loves and desires—career advancement, philosophical curiosity, and licentious

---

8. Lewis, *Four Loves*, 113–15.
9. Lewis, *Screwtape Letters*, in *Signature Classics*, 189, 236, 261.
10. Chesterton, "Ethics of Elfland," in *Orthodoxy*, 42–63.

sexual *eros*—concluded in his famous autobiographical prayer to God, *Confessions*, that "our hearts are restless until they can find peace in You."[11] Margaret Nussbaum describes Augustine's conversion from human passion to a desire for God as "a deeply erotic work, a work filled with expressions of erotic tension and erotic longing. God is addressed throughout in language that Dido might well have used to Aeneas."[12]

Distinct from loving God through the habits of Christian liturgy and worship (*storge*), which emphasizes the collective and public gathering with others in community, the love of God in *eros* lies distinctively in the desire of each self, alone before God, the story of a life journey either away in separation and unlikeness from God or toward union and likeness with him as the source of all life and truth. This is vividly illustrated by two classic works of Christian allegory: the medieval poet Dante in his imaginative tour through the deepest pits of hell's eternal ugliness, upward through the transitory and correctional disciplines of Mount Purgatory, and finally through the heavens into the perfect fulfillment of desire in the paradisical delights and eternal vision of God's beauty.[13] The Baptist Puritan John Bunyan depicted it as the journey of Christian from the City of Destruction through the wilderness of sin, sorrow, and suffering to the Celestial City.[14] Each person, each soul, has a destiny after this finite, material existence, either in complete separation (hell) or complete and perfect union with God (paradise).

The Christian love of God in *eros* is the one-to-One experience of personal relationship with God, where his existence and presence are known to individuals. Oftentimes, it is expressed as an affective encounter and union with God who brings with it the fruits of love, joy, peace, and pleasure. Desire to grow ever closer to God who is Spirit and not of this world creates a tension with living in this world that—even though created

---

11. Augustine, *Confessions*, 17 (bk. 1, ch. 1).

12. Nussbaum, *Upheavals of Thought*, 528–30.

13. Lewis suggests that our eternal destination will in some manner be the natural extension and fulfillment of godly desires and loves (dispositions) on earth. If heaven and what it is about is not desired and loved on earth, then heaven would not be a place such a person could ever feel at home. Lewis, *Great Divorce*, in *Signature Classics*, 463–542. See also his discussion of those in hell who are "self-enslaved," who will not relinquish their freedom even there. Lewis, *Problem of Pain*, in *Signature Classics*, 620–27. The spirit of Satan (and those in hell) proclaim: "Better to reign in Hell than serve in Heav'n." Milton, *Paradise Lost*, 12 (book 1, line 263).

14. Bunyan, *Pilgrim's Progress*.

good—is not spirit and not God. Where *philia* involves loving God through use of the mortal body in the active life of sacrificial, self-giving love for the world, *eros* is the desire of the self for the experience of direct communion with God, often by means of withdrawal from the world in contemplation, prayer, and studious meditation on Scripture. There is a long tradition of mysticism in historical Christianity that emphasizes this individual union of the soul with God, touching his eternal spirit that lives from beyond the realm of material senses.

This experience should be nurtured and sustained through liturgical habits of communal worship (*storge*) and should overflow into friendship with Christ (*philia*), but taken to excess on its own, throughout the Christian centuries, loving God in *eros* has also led to tendencies that diminish the importance of liturgical worship, isolate the self, and that scorn the world. As discussed above, Lewis defines human *eros* as a "delighted preoccupation," an admiration and adoration so forceful that cannot be satisfied with a mere distant Appreciative-love but desires full attachment, possession, and union—to remove all distance between the lover and the beloved, making them one. *Eros*'s greatest strength is desire—its willingness to suffer loss for the sake of the beloved—and also its greatest weakness. *Eros* can become its own objective (an end rather than a means), and thus a god. Desire for God becomes desire for the feeling of desire. The individual focus may also become so exclusive and possessive that it jealously ignores everything and everyone else around it—like two lovers lost in each other's gaze.[15]

Like his warnings about banking too much on human *eros* in *The Four Loves*, Lewis once responded to a woman's letter, urging her not to rely too much on the excitement and "sensations" of her new religious commitment:

> It is not the sensations that are the real thing. . . . Don't depend on them. Otherwise when they go and you are once more emotionally flat (as you certainly will be quite soon), you might think that the real thing had gone too. But it won't. It will be there when you can't feel it. May even be most operative when you can feel it least. . . . Excitement, of whatever sort, never lasts. . . . So enjoy the push while it lasts, but enjoy it as a treat, not as something normal.[16]

---

15. See Lewis's comparison of friendship love (*philia*) and romantic desire (*eros*) in *Four Loves*, 61.

16. Lewis to Mrs. Sonia Graham, May 15, 1952, in *Letters of C. S. Lewis*, 539-40.

For Lewis, Christian discipleship was ultimately more an "affair of the will" than emotions or "devout feelings," which come and go,[17] and its health was preserved in other ways than much sought-after spiritual visions or ecstatic experiences. Rather, Christianity is sustained by the habits of devotion to the word and religious readings, the liturgy of the church, and in the inspiration of spiritual friendship.[18] As with *philia*, Lewis does not develop *eros* as an image of loving God to any significant degree in *The Four Loves*, but he was well versed in Christian mysticism, both Western and Eastern writers, and his writings arguably express Platonic and Augustinian emphases on ultimate desire. His definition of human *eros* fits well within his own general characterization of Christianity as ultimately a desire for God, a deep hunger for uncreated pleasure unending in him,[19] which serves as a significant apologetic for the Christian supernatural worldview. As good as creation is, it is merely a lesser delight, or a partial and limited fulfillment of desire, whereas God and heaven are the ultimate delight and infinite fulfillment of all creaturely desire. "We are half-hearted creatures, fooling about with drink and sex and ambition when infinite joy is offered to us, like an ignorant child who wants to go on making mud pies in the slum because he cannot imagine what is meant by the offer of a holiday at the sea. We are far too easily pleased."[20]

Latin and Byzantine Ascetical Spirituality

Limitations or deficiencies in the organized church, a higher spiritual status associated with those in the ordained priesthood, and the dominance of liturgical rites of the church as mediating access to God: these realities prompted many movements in historical Christianity that emphasized a more direct, unmediated encounter and personal relationship with God. Such movements in history have a range of intentions and contexts, but all illustrate a common stress placed on loving God as the experience of personal *eros*, an affection-producing encounter of spiritual union. Along with the pursuit of intellectual knowledge in the growth of medieval scholasticism and universities, mystical movements often arose in reaction to

17. Lewis, *Mere Christianity*, in *Signature Classics*, 111.
18. Downing, *Region of Awe*, 159–61.
19. Gaddy, *Love Affair with God*, 56–57.
20. Lewis, "Weight of Glory," in *Weight of Glory*, 2, 13–14; Armstrong, *Medieval Wisdom*, 167–70.

religious contexts that appeared to place excessive stress on loving God as outward participation in liturgical worship and conformity to the moral norms of society, distorting true *storge* and *philia*.

Even before Christianity was legalized and then became the state-established religion in the later fourth century, there was already a movement of desert-dwelling Christian men and women in Egypt that sought to pull away in literal likeness to Christ from worldly attachments and accumulation of material pleasures to discipline their bodies, devote themselves to contemplative prayer, and experience as close a union with the infinite and pure Spirit of God as possible in a finite, mortal world.

Unlike other creatures, humans uniquely were created with both a material nature and an immaterial nature. As Lewis states in his first work of Christian fiction, *Pilgrim's Regress*, "We were made to be neither cerebral men nor visceral men, but Men. Not beasts nor angels but Men—things at once rational and animal."[21] After the fall, those natures now exist in tension and pull individuals in opposite directions, and in the mind of the monastic tradition, one could not grow simultaneously in greater union and love with the immaterial and perfect God while also growing in greater union and love with the finite, material, and imperfect world. Did not Scripture teach that prosperity and luxury leads to indifference of God and righteousness (Matt 19:24), that bodily suffering produces character and hope (Rom 5:3–5), and that really the only part of human anthropology that can move *away* from degeneration is the human spirit (2 Cor 4:16)? Faith is tested and love is proven by suffering, as Jesus himself modeled in his passion. What monastics did was to *choose* suffering voluntarily, a sort of self-inflicted martyrdom and testing of their faith, but not suffering for its own sake. Christian "asceticism" (a word associated with athletic discipline) was born from a desire to experience union with God, a path believed to pass needfully through self-denial, sacrifice, and suffering, which both encourages and is encouraged by prayer and spiritual contemplation.

Antony was the father of Christian hermit monasticism in the third century, and his life was written by the Council of Nicaea's leading theological advocate, Athanasius, bishop of Alexandria.[22] The martyrs of earlier Roman persecution were esteemed for their sacrifice of life and limb for the love of God and were honored to follow the way of their crucified Savior. Such was the model of life that inspired the burst of monasticism's

---

21. Lewis, *Pilgrim's Regress*, 215.
22. Athanasius, *Life of Antony*.

growth, especially after Christianity became legally protected, patronized, and prosperous. In the eyes of the men and women desert monks, the new age of cultural Christianity and complacent faith was answered by the call of testing in the wilderness.

It was the ascetic and monastic traditions of the Western and Eastern churches that fed much of the love of God as *eros* in the early and medieval history of Christianity.[23] Among the ancient Christian fathers, like Origen, Lactantius, Gregory of Nyssa, Augustine, and Maximus the Confessor, union with God ("seeing" his face) is the consummation of human desire and delight of the soul. Synthesizing Platonic metaphysics and an Aristotelian ontology of motion, infinite happiness is found only in the pursuit of knowing God who transcends the finite world. This is accomplished not through mere intellectual knowledge (natural philosophy or biblical study), but a passion or desire of the heart to possess God in union, an emotional affection for God's Beauty that draws (i.e., moves) the soul like the force of gravity into knowing God in a mystical, experiential union of adoration and love.[24]

This emphasis on affection-for-the-infinite was carried forward into medieval times in Boethius's *Consolation of Philosophy*,[25] the prayers of Anselm, Bernard of Clairvaux's *On Loving God*, and Bonaventura's *On the Mind's Road to God*. These writings express the vaporous happiness experienced in finite things and that the *telos* of life both now and hereafter is one and the same: experiencing peace in union with God and the merging of human and divine hearts and wills perfectly in love. This involves forsaking pride and vanity, voluntary self-restraint and repression of mortal attachments, lusts, and all distractions from the path of virtue (moral philosophy), as well as faithfully accepting all sufferings not within one's control. Asceticism is the means for clearing the sight of the mind and heart to focus on prayerful contemplation of God and union with the glory of his presence

---

23. For an overview of the affective tradition in ancient and medieval Christianity, see Armstrong, *Medieval Wisdom*, 170–86. (Interestingly, Armstrong even draws a connection between Lewis and Platonic definitions of *eros* but does not significantly develop any related application of the *The Four Loves*.)

24. Wilken, *Early Christian Thought*, 291–311.

25. Defining happiness as the natural goal sought by humanity, following Aristotle, Boethius in dialogue with Lady Philosophy learns that "there is a certain imperfect happiness in perishable good, so that there can be no doubt that a true and perfect happiness exists." Boethius, *Consolation of Philosophy*, 99 (bk. 3, ch. 10). This is echoed later by Lewis, who was an admirer of this work.

in the self, in the natural world (natural philosophy), and ultimately God himself revealed as infinite Trinity (theology). There is a moment reached at which the ascent of self-conscious knowing stops and God is immediately and intuitively felt beyond deliberate thought. This is the height and pinnacle of mystical union running throughout the medieval writers and in the Renaissance humanist revival of Platonism in the Western Catholic tradition. Following purity of mind and body through moral philosophy and dialectical reasoning (involving a synthesis of liberal arts and Christian, Jewish, and pagan writings), the Italian Renaissance humanist Pico della Mirandola described being "smitten by the ineffable love as by a sting, and, like the Seraphim, born outside ourselves, filled with the godhead, we shall be, no longer ourselves, but the very One who made us."[26]

The Dominican friar and theologian Thomas Aquinas described happiness, a human's ultimate end, as the individual contemplation of God. While in Catholic thought it is grace-infused moral habits (faith formed by love) that are *the means* to approaching likeness to God, and therefore acceptance into the glorious vision of God, happiness and pleasure (*eudaimonia*) in God—rather than doing good—are the ultimate *ends* of human life.[27] Glimpses of that glory can even be experienced in this life, according to the divine encounters described in the lives of Moses, Elijah, and Paul. Before the age of modern science that downplayed or denied the supernatural and miraculous, it was believable that others, in conformity to Christ through ascetic discipline and contemplation, could and did experience a rare and special visionary union with God. Two great aesthetes of the medieval period, though differing in the vocational paths they took, are believed to have reached these summits. For Francis of Assisi (founder of the Franciscan Order approved by the pope in 1209), to know God was less a thing of the mind and more of a "romance" and "love affair," whose wildness was seen in his approach to living an extraordinary life amid the ordinary. While Thomas Aquinas reflected philosophically on the nature

---

26. Pico della Mirandola, *Oration*, 25–27.

27. Aristotle long ago determined philosophically that the ultimate end of human beings is happiness achieved through the virtuous, disciplined life of moderation between extremes. Aristotle, *Nichomachean Ethics*. Aquinas defined happiness, our "ultimate end" and "good," in terms of contemplative union with God, which is aided by the cooperation of grace with moral discipline and virtue. Aquinas, *Selected Writings*, 508–9, 517. This is a significant contrast with modern liberal and secular humanism, which views the pleasurable benefits of improved social conditions as the ultimate end confined to the present life and world. Taylor, *Secular Age*, 221.

of man, Francis was busily ministering to real men—poor and neglected lepers to be exact. While Thomas was, as a Christian student of Aristotle, fascinated by natural science, Francis could be found in the woods preaching to birds. Yet, it is claimed that both later in life experienced encounters of mystical union with God where the veiled glory of the supernatural was seen in ways that had a rare, physical effect on both men. Aquinas is believed to have heard God's clear voice emanating from a crucifix, and in another moment following deep contemplation of the Eucharist he is said to have levitated in the sight of other friars. Francis of Assisi was believed to have received the stigmata (wounds of Christ) in his hands and feet following a rapturous vision of a winged heavenly being.[28]

In the Latin West, it was common for ascetic mystics to describe loving desire and union with God using highly erotic imagery and language, including and especially by female mystics such as Teresa of Avila, Catherine of Siena, and (C. S. Lewis's favorite) Julian of Norwich.[29] The Song of Songs (Solomon), which for many ancient and medieval Christians appeared scandalous if really celebrating human romance and erotic sexuality, was interpreted as an allegory of spiritual intimacy and union with God. From Origen of Alexandria and running through medieval theology in Pope Gregory and Bernard of Clairvaux (who preached for eighteen years on the Song of Songs),[30] the pleasures of sexual union and romantic love were seen as a weaker and baser form of the greater spiritual romance and ecstasy to be experienced in an individual's love union with God in mystical contemplation.[31]

Spiritual visions accompanied experiences of contemplation, rewarding the soul's desire for union with God's being and love. The Lord showed Julian of Norwich a vision of a hazel nut in the palm of her hand, which represented all creation, reassuring her that all things last which are beloved of God and that in him she is to find her rest: "This is the cause why we be not all in ease of heart and soul: that we seek here rest in those things

---

28. Chesterton, *St. Thomas Aquinas*, 32, 67–68, 112, 176.

29. Jaegher, *Anthology of Christian Mysticism*; Armstrong, *Medieval Wisdom*, 179–82.

30. Armstrong, *Medieval Wisdom*, 171, 173, 175; Bernard, *Selected Works*, 207–78.

31. Armstrong, *Medieval Wisdom*, 183; Leiva-Merikakis, *Love's Sacred Order*, 116–24. On the union of the human spirit with the Spirit of God who dwells within the soul as a "spiritual marriage," see also Teresa of Avila, *Interior Castle*, 269–70. Dante meets "Beatrice" in Paradise, a woman he adored on earth but who was now to guide him toward the greatest fulfillment of all love—God. Dante, *Paradiso*, 15 (canto 2, lines 19–30); Nussbaum, *Upheavals of Thought*, 557–90.

that be so little, wherein is no rest, and know not our God that is Almighty, All-wise, and All-good."[32] The sixteenth-century Spanish mystic Teresa of Avila describes the vision of a castle made of seven dwellings granted to her by Jesus as a way of symbolizing that the way to communion with God in the soul was increasing dedication to humility, physical self-discipline, and contemplative prayer.[33] At the same time, these rapturous experiences are momentary gifts (blessings) of God's grace, and like passionate human lovers separated from each other, there is ignited such a longing for unending communion with God in the soul and a detachment (even contempt) for created things that this is experienced now as a desperate pain that can even be hazardous to bodily health.[34]

Late medieval and early modern mystics also testify of physical responses to these blessed moments of intensified soul communion with God. Catherine of Siena recounts feeling as if she had left her body, but a revelation from Jesus instructed her that she merely lost consciousness of her surroundings through heightened focus upon his love: "The memory is full of nothing but Me; the intellect, elevated, gazes upon the object of My Truth; the affection, which follows the intellect, loves and becomes united with that which the intellect sees. These powers, being united and gathered together and immersed in Me, the body loses its feeling, so that the seeing eye sees not, and the hearing ear hears not, and the tongue does not speak."[35] The English mystic Richard Rolle wrote romantic ballads to Christ and spoke of a literal feeling of physical heat in his chest and the hearing of heavenly music during heights of contemplation.[36]

Western mysticism flourished in the late Middle Ages and often was a reaction to what was perceived as excessive reliance on liturgical rituals and intellectual and rational disputations over theology in university scholasticism. Although it often claimed no intention to undermine existing authorities or knowledge, the fact that it offered unmediated encounters with and revelations from God to morally self-restrained and contemplative individuals—and not just the priestly clergy who administrate

---

32. Jaegher, *Anthology of Christian Mysticism*, 57–58.

33. Teresa of Avila, *Interior Castle*. A popular devotional among evangelicals written in the form of extra-biblical, personal messages from Jesus is Sarah Young's *Jesus Calling*.

34. Teresa of Avila, *Interior Castle*, 248–55. On the unattainability of satisfying our spiritual longings for perfect and permanent union with God in this life, see Nussbaum's discussion of Augustine in *Upheavals of Thought*, 545.

35. Jaegher, *Anthology of Christian Mysticism*, 69.

36. Rolle, *Fire of Love*.

the sacraments, the educated in the universities, or those who had taken monastic vows—inevitably invoked suspicion and antagonism toward currents of mysticism.

There were varieties of mystical approach in the Middle Ages, ranging from more to less orthodox. Cistercian, Franciscan, and Modern Devotion (Brethren of Common Life) movements stressed contemplation and imitation of the life and passion of Jesus.[37] Others were more devoted to contemplating the presence and union of God's Spirit within oneself, and in the case of the controversial German mystic Meister Eckhart, to the abolishing of all divine-human distinctions, viewing the self as essentially a pre-existent emanation of God's very being.[38]

Mainstream monasticism that flourished in the Greek East was more exclusively mystical in orientation than in the Western Latin Church. Whereas the West developed a concurrent rational tradition in the rise of the universities in the 1200s, theological expression in Imperial Eastern Christianity remained much more focused on experiences of contemplative prayer and the habits of liturgical worship.[39] In fact, in a highly influential work *Mystical Theology* that dates to the fifth century by Pseudo-Dionysius the Aeropagite, union with God is characterized in terms of *unknowing*, or the *via negativa*.[40] As God dwells in mystery and unapproachable light (1 Tim 1:16), which to the mind and spiritual eyes of finite and fallen creatures is blinding as darkness, God is beyond the ability of mental concepts or words to capture him. Thus, the purest way to approach God in union is in silence, through rhythmic breathing, and hesychast prayer (like the popular Orthodox prayer "Jesus Christ, Son of David Have Mercy on Me"), emptying the mind of all that is *not* God:

> The fact is that the more we take flight upward, the more our words are confined to the ideas we are capable of forming; so that now as we plunge into that darkness which is beyond intellect, we shall find ourselves not simply running short of words but actually speechless and unknowing. . . . The more language falters, and when it has passed up and beyond the ascent, it will turn

---

37. See the classic work of the Modern Devotion movement, Thomas à Kempis, *Imitation of Christ*.

38. Ozment, *Age of Reform*, 115–34.

39. Payton, *Light from the Christian East*, 57–68.

40. A counterpart to this work in the Western tradition was the anonymous English work *The Cloud of Unknowing*. Jaegher, *Anthology of Christian Mysticism*, 42–48.

silent completely, since it will finally be at one with him who is indescribable.[41]

Mysticism in the Protestant Reformation

Mystical emphasis on interior communication and union with God continued to challenge Roman Catholic institutional structures in the rise of the movement of Quietism and in the writings of Madame Guyon in the late 1600s and early 1700s. Guyon's confidence in the extreme union of God and the soul through contemplative prayer to the point of dissolving the individual self totally possessed by God landed her in prison in 1695.[42]

Guyon was parallel with a turn to mystical emphasis among the heirs of Protestantism in the late seventeenth century. The Protestant Reformation heritage rejected monastic vows as lacking explicit biblical warrant, for their extremity in ascetic suppression of bodily and worldly good, and for their proneness to self-effort and works-righteousness, as if such practice fit the soul to be received in heaven and see God. Martin Luther early on translated a work by the German mystic John Tauler, as it challenged the privileged relationship with God claimed by the ordained papal and episcopal hierarchy. However, Luther came to reject mysticism in the sense that it stressed union with and likeness to God as more through human effort in asceticism, prayer, and contemplation rather than approaching God through faith in his gift of total righteousness in Christ.[43]

However, by the late 1600s, a movement arose within German Lutheranism, quite similar and even drawing from the medieval Catholic mystical tradition, that once again stressed a more personal, experiential relationship with God (*eros*) over against excessive equation of being true Christians with Lutheranism in theological knowledge and conformity to

---

41. Pseudo-Dionysius, "Mystical Theology," 217–18. Ironically, however, medieval Greek Christians debated whether the ecstatic experience of union with God and vision of his light was of God himself or his emanations/energies. Ware, *Orthodox Church*, 64–70.

42. Guyon, "Spiritual Torrents," 245–49.

43. Moltmann, *Crucified God*, 213. So, in Luther's theology of justification, we are not transformed by grace into righteousness and thereby made perfect and fit to see the Lord in heaven, but sinners are justified now and enter heaven in the future only by believing in the mercy of God in Christ's righteousness alone. Yet through faith the righteous Christ is also present in us through the Holy Spirit. On justification as union with God, see Mannermaa and Stjerna, *Christ Present in Faith*.

liturgical rituals and ceremonies (*storge*). It also developed out of the wake of destructive doctrinal controversies that divided the churches and states of Europe in the tumultuous Thirty Years' War (1618–48).[44] A new wave of *Protestant* mysticism emerged in the later generations of the institutionalized Reformation.

For Lutheran mystics like Johann Arndt, true Christianity is a love union with God that awakens inward affections by the Spirit and that bears the fruit of obedience in likeness to Christ. Pietists such as Philip Jakob Spener continued to argue for the importance of academic theological training for ordained ministers, but the movement also leaned toward a more universalizing stress on Christianity as ultimately the inward transformation of desires, affections, and moral inclinations through spiritual union with the indwelling Holy Spirit.[45] Pietist devotional writings reflect a poetic love to God as the true lover of the soul in almost romantic, quasi-erotic language that echoes the medieval mystical traditions:

> I count the hours, days and years,
> And time seems never-ending until I completely Embrace you, o life.
> Then what is mortal in me will be completely swallowed up in you, and I will be
> immortal. With the fire of love My heart glows so that it ignites What is in me,
> and my mind binds itself so to you. That you in me and I in you, And I yet always
> more will press nearer into you.[46]

> Air, which feels all, in which we always move, Ground and life of all things,
> Sea without bottom or end, Miracle of all Miracles,
> I sink into you, I in you, you in me. Let me completely disappear, find and see only you.[47]

---

44. The other reaction to this state of religious tension in Europe helped give birth to Enlightenment rationalism. See McGrath, *Christian History*, 211–12, 214–20.

45. Zinzendorf's Moravians were instructed not to proselytize in favor of any denomination but to be a unifying, renewal movement among all denominations, enlivening them with a heart devotion to the crucified Christ and one another in love. Lewis, *Zinzendorf*, 124–33.

46. See the song authored by German Pietist August Hermann Francke in Freylinghuasen's "Spiritual Songbook, 1705," in Erb, *Pietists*, 173.

47. Tersteegen, "Spiritual Flower Garden," in Erb, *Pietists*, 251.

Eros

For all their emphasis on a personal experience of love union with God, German and Moravian Pietists sought to maintain the importance of loving God through liturgical worship, but other movements of Anabaptist Spiritualism went even further to diminish or radically negate as erroneous and un-Christian *all* organized liturgical ceremonies and use of outward symbols:

> I am thus quite convinced now that for fourteen hundred years now there has existed no gathered church nor any sacrament.... The church is today a purely spiritual thing.... Therefore, the unitary Spirit alone baptizes with fire and the Spirit all the faithful and [all] who are obedient to the inner Word in whatever part of the world they be.... So long as they retain the light which has shined upon them and gives their heart an eternal glow.... I maintain against all ecclesiastical authorities that all outward things and ceremonies, which were customary in the church of the apostles, have been done away with and are not to be reinstated.[48]

The Salesian nobleman and lay theologian Caspar Schwenkfeld stopped participating in the Lord's Supper altogether after 1526 due to his emphasis on the true partaking of the Lord's Supper as purely inward, spiritual, or mystical.[49] Similarly, George Fox and the movement known as Friends (or Quakers), begun in the 1650s amid the religious turbulence of seventeenth-century Civil-War England, stressed the universal sharing of God's Inner Light in egalitarian worship meetings without any programmed order of service or use of outward sacramental practices. Meetings involving extended periods of silence were open to spontaneous, immediate, and direct (and in their minds more authentic) impressions and movements of the Holy Spirit as he spoke to each person individually (men *and* women) to lead with a word of exhortation, prayer, or song.[50]

Anne Hutchinson was at the center of controversy that nearly split the Massachusetts Bay Colony in the 1630s. Whether it was her theology or her gender that made her more of an enemy of the male Puritan establishment, Hutchinson was viewed as a schismatic threat to the religious,

---

48. Francke, "Letter to John Campanus," in Williams, *Spiritual and Anabaptist Writers*, 149–50.

49. Schwenkfeld, "An Answer to Luther's Malediction," in Williams, *Spiritual and Anabaptist Writers*, 161–62.

50. Durham, *Spirit of the Quakers*, 19–40; White, *Protestant Worship*, 135–41. Although nothing was prescribed or prepared beforehand, meetings still (generally) included the rudiment parts of a Christian liturgy: prayers, songs, exhortation.

moral, and social cohesion of the colony administrated by the clerical and civil authorities. Her appeal to the personal teaching of the Holy Spirit was expressed through teaching female and male guests in her home, which included her opinions on immediate and full assurance of salvation apart from all evidence in works. Not surprisingly, Hutchinson was not welcome in Massachusetts and found acceptance in Rhode Island, which, under another expelled Puritan, Baptist Roger Williams, was among the few colonies allowing for wider religious liberty in North America on the principle of true spiritual religion being primarily a personal and inward-proceeding dynamic.[51]

American Revivalism and Pentecostal-Charismatic Movements

British and American Protestant revivalism of the eighteenth century, much like the continental German Pietism of Spener and Francke, sought to awaken congregations by stressing the need for a personal, spiritual experience of God that stoked the fires of inward affections. Earlier movements of Puritanism and Pietism, which elevated the intensity of personal devotion, fed into the spiritual awakenings of a new century led by itinerant preachers such as Anglican clergymen John Wesley and George Whitfield. Although not anti-liturgical to the extreme of Quakerism, the emotional enthusiasm of revival services in colonial New England in the 1730s and 40s was criticized by "Old Light" churchmen, splitting churches of various Protestant denominations. Tradition-minded clergy considered the outdoor preaching, urgent pleading for the new birth, and excessive excitement of the revivalist meetings as a challenge to the status of their own leadership, and evangelical claims of seeing dreams and visions and emotional outbursts in crying, dancing, and swooning were viewed as improper behavior disruptive to the liturgical order. Revivalists countered that empty attachment to hierarchical, organized tradition and the lack of expressive feeling, a modern form of Pharisaical religion (excessive *storge*), was the sign of unconverted souls and the cause behind the spiritual and moral malaise of New England populations.[52] Congregationalist pastor Jonathan

---

51. MacHaffie, *Her Story*, 80–82. Roger Williams was only a Baptist for several months before identifying as an independent religious seeker like George Fox (before founding the Friends).

52. Kidd, *America's Religious History*, 32–42; Sweeney, *American Evangelical Story*, 27–61; Noll et al., *Turning Points*, 199–221.

Edwards penned his book, *Religious Affections* (1746), to defend the revival movement and to argue that there is no "true religion" without the engagement and arousing of the inward affections of the heart—love, desire, joy, etc. (*eros*).[53] Strong emphases on Christianity as the experience of divine *eudaimonia* (pleasure) are evident in today's Calvinist heirs of Edwards, especially in the popular writings of Baptist pastor John Piper.[54] Echoing the Presbyterian *Westminster Confession of Faith* (1647), humanity was created ultimately to "know and *enjoy* the pleasure of God," impressing that the primary activity for the Christian life on earth and the hope of heaven is experiential delight through individual fixation on the beauty and glory of God.[55]

With roots in the Methodist-Holiness renewal movement of the late nineteenth century (including Wesleyan Methodism and the Church of the Nazarene), the birth of American Pentecostalism added to the personal spiritual encounter with God the bestowing of a second gift of the Holy Spirit after conversion. Whereas Holiness and Keswick preachers stressed this as a moment of greater love and surrender to God in holiness, Pentecostalism added manifestations of spiritual power in speaking in tongues, miraculous healings, uncontrolled fainting, dancing, and holy laughter. The Azusa Street Revival that exploded for three and a half years within Los Angeles's Apostolic Faith Mission and pastored by African American preacher William J. Seymour in 1906 broke down racial and gender barriers and provided many from among the lower classes with the opportunity to feel and express an experience of dramatic spiritual empowerment—a further democratization of Christian worship and intensifying of supernatural encounter in an age increasingly defined by modern science. Much like other manifestations of revival in previous centuries, Azusa was not without its detractors for its excessive enthusiasm and more chaotic worship services that could be heard blocks away (including some local occultists who came to participate), but Seymour's ministry went on to influence the emergence and development of Pentecostal denominations such as the largely black Church of God in Christ (COGIC) and its segregationist daughter

---

53. Edwards, "Religious Affections," 143, 145.

54. Piper, *Desiring God*.

55. In contrast, there are some who stress a more Jewish-Christian understanding of salvation in terms of heaven's future coming to the new earth (Rev 21), which will include a perfection of balanced worship *and* creative work. Middleton, *New Heaven and Earth*. For how this impacts our active Christian life in the present, see Wright, *Simply Christian*, 222–28.

the Assemblies of God (AG) established in 1914. From its small origins, Pentecostalism has gone on to become the largest global manifestation of Christianity today.[56]

A charismatic wave, also emerging from California in the 1960s to 1980s, went on to influence nearly all Protestant denominations and even renewal of some Roman Catholic churches. While not adopting the Pentecostal necessity of speaking in tongues as a sign of a second blessing from the Holy Spirit, the charismatic movement celebrated tongues and other gifts of immediate supernatural blessing as evidence of divine encounter. John Wimber of Fuller Theological Seminary and Vineyard Christian Fellowship were especially influential in introducing more emotionally expressive and contemporary styles of worship across various denominations, probably the principal way that the charismatic movement has made its mark across the American Protestant evangelical movement since the 1980s and 90s.[57]

Spiritual *Eros*: Need and Excess

Even though this chapter is devoted to the individual's experience of God in *eros*, it can be argued that the modern liturgies of contemporary Christian worship are arguably over-individualized. How many worship songs speak of "I" and "me" more than "we" and "us"? Worship leaders will often encourage people as individuals in the congregation to express themselves, so that even the public assembling together for worship has become another place to experience individual connection with God. As Alistair Roberts notes,

> As meaning is relocated from the external and social world into the private and buffered world of the individual mind, our experience of Christian liturgy shifts, and the locus of its meaning is dispersed. Although we may continue to practice the liturgy as a common and collective rite, like a large pond that has steadily drained out through hundreds of plug holds, its meaning now

---

56. Sweeney, *American Evangelical Story*, 142–49; Synan, *Holiness-Pentecostal Tradition*, 97–106, 153–56, 279–81; Cox, *Fire From Heaven*; Sunquist, *Unexpected Christian Century*, 79–83. On the global growth of Pentecostalism and its particular emphasis on healings as power encounters over demonic forces, see Jenkins, *Next Christendom*, 124–31; Jenkins, *New Faces*, 113–24.

57. Synan, *Holiness-Pentecostal Tradition*, 253–78.

increasingly resides in the privacy of worshipers' minds, rather than in the shared space and action that unites us.[58]

Not that this is all bad. The eighteenth-century revivalists also had each personal soul in sight in their calls to respond to the preached word in repentance and faith (even if the actual working of the Spirit of God in Calvinism was limited to the secret elect). Higher liturgical churches, by contrast, practiced public confession of sins more collectively in unison as a community. This break in modern evangelical liturgies assumed that both could not coexist, unrecognizing the degree to which individual sin before God also impacts the collective sin of the local worshiping community before God—as Jesus addressed the *churches* of Asia in Revelation chapters 2 and 3. The same could be said of sharing in the Lord's Supper, which has also become individualized in modern evangelical worship.[59] It should be a deeply personal moment (*eros* with *storge*), and yet there is a reason why it is to be celebrated collectively and publicly in community, not only because participating in the symbolic action together reminds Christians that they share together in thanksgiving for the Lord's salvation but that the people of God are not only individuals responsible to God but as local communities as well.

The desire for a personal, spiritual experience of God, manifested in miracles or generating emotional pleasure, is appealing to a modern culture that puts a heavy premium not only on individual experience and responsibility but on feelings. As such, the arousal and presence of feelings are often seen as the seat of authentic Christianity for younger people. One often hears of a young believer "falling" or "being in love with Jesus." This, in part, reflects an adolescent idealization of romance, which has made its own impact on liturgical reforms to appeal to younger generations in the later twentieth century. Many modern worship lyrics read like romantic love letters, emphasizing deep feelings of spiritual longing and desire, including those that, taken out of their ecclesial context, could be mistaken for songs about a human romance. Praise songs such as "Nothing Else" are highly individualized (using words like "I" and "my"), are set to emotionally soothing or thrilling, anthemic pop and rock melodies, and use evocative, romantic language (and rather boastful claims of absolute love and devotion) to express the soul's one desire to remain emotionally transfixed on God.

58. Roberts, *Liturgical Piety*, 66.
59. Roberts, *Liturgical Piety*, 66.

Younger Christians typically look down upon older generations and forms of Christian worship, which had used musical forms suitable to their *own* time and culture, now as empty rituals that lack emotional arousal and expression. As Thomas Bergler, in *The Juvenilization of American Christianity*, observes,

> Adolescent Christians see the faith as incomplete unless it is affecting them emotionally. They are less likely than adults to settle for a faith that offers only a dutiful adherence to particular doctrines, rules, or institutions. On the other hand, they have a hard time keeping religious commitments when their emotions are not cooperating. They are drawn to religious practices that produce emotional highs and sometimes assume that experiencing strong feelings is the same thing as spiritual authenticity. They may be tempted to believe that God's main role in their lives is to help them feel better or to heal their emotional pain. Juvenalized adults agree that a main purpose of Christianity is to help them feel better about their problems.[60]

A spiritual hunger to know and experience God personally and in emotionally satisfying ways has a long tradition in biblical and Christian history. Nineteenth-century Romanticism and American Protestant revivalism did not invent this. The Hebrew Psalms often express such individual and emotional desperation for God. The Pentecostal desire to experience union with God in manifestations of supernatural power, the child of nineteenth-century frontier evangelical revivalism, shares a likeness with the spiritual intimacy craved by Catholic mystics, both of which claimed prophetic visions and abnormal bodily reactions (even levitation!).[61]

The Pentecostal and charismatic movements and their influence on modern evangelical approaches to worship merely accentuated the prominent place of spiritual experience in the history of Catholic mysticism and Protestant revivalism, adding freedom for dancing, tongues speaking, and the promise of miraculous healings as a renewal of the Holy Spirit's dynamic power among the worshiping congregation reminiscent of the apostolic New Testament age.[62] This might have been more generally welcomed by

---

60. Bergler, *Juvenilization of American Christianity*, 9, 12, 220–21, 224–29. Bergler discusses juvenilization, the experience of an emotionally fulfilling and passionate faith, and a particular cultural form of American Christianity, in terms of both its benefits and costs.

61. Chan, *Pentecostal Theology*, 82–83; Teresa of Avila, *Interior Castle*, 195–96.

62. Meeks argues that modern expressions of charismatic spontaneity in Pentecostal

evangelicals if not carried to the excesses of modern prosperity gospels or chaotic worship services that focus on satisfying people hungry to feel better or desire an experience of supernatural miracles. This crosses the line into what charismatic church leaders have often accused of older traditional liturgies—human efforts to manipulate the presence and work of God. Furthermore, with their emphasis on what Chan refers to as the "radical in-breaking of the Spirit" and an "over-realized eschatology," Pentecostal and charismatic-style worship faces greater difficulties reconciling spiritual growth—as the medieval mystics understood—with necessary seasons of "spiritual aridity," "desolation," and "dark nights of the soul."[63] Pentecostal, charismatic, and liturgical forms of worship, however, need not be viewed as complete contraries, as if Christians are forced to have to choose between more reverent and liturgical and more emotionally expressive, charismatic services. Rather, an opportunity exists for more mutual revitalization,[64] remembering late medieval Catholic mystics who devotedly attended High Mass, German and Moravian Pietists who continued worshiping in the established Lutheran Church, and the influence of charismatic expressions on contemporary liturgies in some Roman Catholic and Messianic Jewish churches.

As Lewis describes in relationship to human love, *eros* makes great boasts but cannot itself fulfill them, and *eros* fades in and out. The danger when it comes to the love of God in *eros* is when *eros* becomes excessive, its own god, and thus a demon. Are people looking to Christ merely as a therapeutical antidote for their emotional ennui? Are they coming to Christ just to escape the tedium of modern life and from a thirst for supernatural experience? Is it possible to misconstrue an affectionate encounter with God, whether in private devotion or public worship, simply because of the way it leaves people *feeling* better? After all, the same people can leave a theme park, a movie, or listening to secular music *feeling* better. As Edwards stated in distinguishing true from false affections, "Such effects [on the body] oftentimes arise from great affections about temporal things

---

worship, similar to first- and second-century Christian practice, do not necessarily preclude the formality of ritual, as the former are "often triggered at predictable times" during the worship service. Meeks, "Grammar of Christian Practice," 101.

63. Chan, *Pentecostal Theology*, 37.

64. Chan, *Pentecostal Theology*, 117–18.

... great affections about secular things that are purely natural, may have these effects."[65]

In the context of a contemporary worship service, is it really the power of the biblically grounded lyrics, the exaltation of the character of God, or is it the pleasure of the lush music on our senses, that is doing *most* of the stirring of affections?[66] Bergler asks, "Is the music we sing in church fostering a self-centered, romantic spirituality in which following Jesus is compared to 'falling in love'? If so, we should not be surprised if some Christians have a relationship with Jesus that has all the maturity and staying power of an adolescent infatuation."[67] Why does it seem that spiritual attention and enthusiasm often fade after the music stops and the word is opened to be preached? Did that pleasurable encounter Christians thought they had with God leave them humbled to live out a stronger commitment to truth, righteousness, selfless sacrifice, purity, patience, mercy, and love—thus to a deeper friendship, or *philia*, suffering with Christ in and for the world?

For Jonathan Edwards, although there is no true religion without the stirring of the affections (*eros*), including those of a degree that have such effects upon the body as to cause fainting during a revival service, not all affections below the surface are the fruit of the Holy Spirit. There are "emotions which made a glaring show" in tears and other "affectionate expressions," which were "in reality nothing." The affections that are truly Christian are those that result in the *practice* of Christian obedience, self-denial, and persevering faithfulness, the "*principal sign*" of sincere godliness for Edwards. In fact, Edwards says that "practice should also be looked upon as the best evidence of friendship towards Christ,"[68] which I have connected with Lewis's definition of *philia*. It is worth quoting Edwards further on the paradoxical necessity yet unreliability of the affections (*eros*):

> Persons in a pang of affection may think they have a willingness of heart for great things, to do much and to suffer much, and so may profess it very earnestly and confidently; when really their

---

65. Edwards, "Religious Affections," 152.

66. Augustine even as far back as the fourth century perceived in his *Confessions* an awareness that the pleasure of musical melodies that stir our moods and affections can mask a weaker devotion to the holy words themselves. See Perl and Kriegsman, "Augustine and Music," 508–9.

67. Bergler, *Juvenilization of American Christianity*, 227; Chan, *Pentecostal Theology*, 75.

68. Edwards, "Religious Affections," 147–52, 164–67; Wilken, *Early Christian Thought*, 297.

hearts are far from it. . . . Passing affections easily produce words; and words are cheap; and godliness is more easily feigned in words than in actions. Christian practice is a costly laborious thing. The self-denial that is required of Christians, and the narrowness of the way that leads to life, don't consist in words, but in practice.[69]

Even the Catholic Carmelite and early modern mystic Teresa of Avila also warned that not every spiritual experience or heightened emotional state is generated from God, and such spiritual experiences are not to be the whole object of a Christian's life. Unlike emphases in much modern Pentecostalism, Teresa discussed how momentary experiences of spiritual absorption in God were also accompanied by spiritual pain, greater *detachment* from and lessening of longing for worldly desires, and a greater obligation to *serve* humbly and selflessly.[70] There is ironically a danger in experiencing extraordinary divine encounters (much like Peter on the Mount of Transfiguration) that leaves hearts wanting more, to stay seated with Mary at Jesus' feet. Mary was affirmed *in that moment* for choosing what was most necessary (Luke 10:42), yet an individual's experience of nearness to the beauty and glory of God also results in his or her being sent and returned to the harsh, broken world to suffer on divine mission for others (Isa 6:1–13; Matt 28:19–20).

It is true that Jesus often withdrew to quiet places to pray (Luke 6:12–13), and Lewis viewed solitude with God in prayer as a given for Christians as taught and demonstrated by their Lord.[71] In an age of incessant visual distraction, Christians today may be less familiar and comfortable with the idea of prolonged solitude and silence, but it can become the space for a daily "conversion," to be the naked self before God where human identity and worth is not determined by others, by worldly prizes, or social expectations, but by God's grace in Jesus Christ alone. In experiencing such acceptance and love in raptures of the heart, indeed it is tempting to want to stay. According to Dante, this is the *telos* of human life in the Beatific Vision in heaven:

> Oh grace abounding that had made me fit
> To fix my eyes on the eternal light until my vision was consumed in it!
> My tranced being stared fixed and motionless upon that vision,

---

69. Edwards, "Religious Affections," 168.

70. Teresa of Avila, *Interior Castle*, 142, 241.

71. Dorsett, *Seeking the Secret Place*, 65; Dorsett, "Lewis and the Care of Souls," 89–100.

> Ever more fervent and motionless upon that vision,
> Ever more fervent to see in the act of seeing.
> Experiencing that Radiance, the spirit
> Is so indrawn it is impossible
> Even to think of ever turning away from it.[72]

Yet it is these experiences that gird up Christians, energizing them to live wisely and faithfully in the messiness of the world through self-giving love for the world in likeness to their Savior.[73] These experiences are meant to refresh and reform, but not to be a permanent dwelling. Craving for spiritual knowledge, a vision, or a feel-good experience can become another form of self-concerned absorption so that it comes to define the essence of the Christian life or love of God,[74] perhaps to the diminishing importance of active ministry of compassion toward the lost, the poor, the sick, and victims of injustice (*philia*). Thus, while the lyrics in the song "Nothing Else" *appear* glorifying to God, expressing a desire for spiritual ascent and to remain transfixed on contemplating his beauty and worth forever, this can in excess slip into a self-interested focus that minimizes union with the heart of God expressed in self-sacrificing *philia*—the mission of humble descent and self-emptying into the world for others modeled in the Incarnation (Phil 2:6–8). Excessive emphasis on the individual self and God, even if nobly focused on experiencing the glory of God, can become twisted into the kind of moral inertia that Chesterton describes concerning some forms of Christian mysticism: "By insisting on the immanence of God we get introspection, self-isolation, quietism, social indifference. . . . Insisting that God is inside man, man is always inside himself."[75] While

---

72. Dante, *Paradiso*, 349–50 (canto 23, lines 82–84, 97–105).

73. See Nouwen, *Way of the Heart*, 19–32.

74. Henri Nouwen points to the ancient desert hermit Antony in Egypt who "concluded his life in total absorption in God. The goal of our life is not people. It is God. Only in him shall we find the rest we seek." Nouwen, *Way of the Heart*, 40. Michael Reeves says that "Christianity is not primarily about lifestyle change; it is about knowing God." Reeves, *Delighting in the Trinity*, 10. Calvinist Baptist pastor John Piper says that "missions exists because worship doesn't." Piper, *Let the Nations Be Glad*, 1. While knowing God and worship for these authors certainly is expected to coincide with the active life of obedience, mission, and service, their statements taken in an excessive way minimizes the active life as subsidiary to "knowing God" and "worship," which is defined primarily as theoretical, contemplative, and liturgical. Rather, there is a unique knowledge of God and worship that also comes reflexively *through* active conformity to the life of Christ in suffering obedience (see Phil 3:10–12).

75. Chesterton, *Orthodoxy*, 141.

sixth-century pope Gregory the Great much preferred the contemplative life, he understood that the soul's retreat with God required his return to the world in spiritual service to others—and vice versa. Shaw summarizes Gregory's understanding of the mixed life: "Complete devotion to the contemplative life is dangerous, as is the pure pursuit of the active life. Good stands in balance and equilibrium, which is achieved when both poles are embraced properly for the good qualities each possesses."[76]

The historical-contextual and theological varieties of the movements described above are widely diverse on a spectrum of doctrinal distinctives. However, their common emphasis on a desire to experience an inward, personal union with God, whether through contemplative prayer and devotional meditation on Scripture (*lectio divina*),[77] or even in the communal worship service, is a pattern that arises throughout the history of Christianity and often as a needed corrective to the excesses of empty or stale *storge* and the independent, overconfident spirit of moral self-righteous *philia*. Loving God as *eros* has resulted in the powerful outpouring of individual sacrifice in both the history of Catholic and Protestant evangelical missions, ministry, and charitable work. This demonstrates that the contemplative life can both ignite and nourish the active life, therefore making it properly a mixed life. Chesterton describes how secular historians speak of Francis of Assisi as "a humanitarian hero" without taking seriously his deep supernatural life, which is trying to "tell the story of a saint without God."[78]

However, when loving God as *eros* becomes excessive or disconnected from the other loves of *storge* and *philia*, it can and has resulted in neglect or indifference toward other equally important expressions of the Christian love of God. Its excess has been known to breed sectarianism, beliefs and practices that boast in a superior personal illumination against the historical Christian consensus, de-emphasizing the significance of Scripture or the need to listen to wise, trained, and skilled biblical teachers of past and present. Those today who claim to "love Jesus" but diminish, or even despise, the organized church depreciate the fact that the same Jesus they love also loves that sinning bride by grace. They also push the valid personal dimension of relationship with God toward dangerous, individualistic extremes that characterize modern subjectivism, theologically vague emotive

---

76. Straw, *Gregory the Great*, 20.

77. Casey, *Sacred Reading*.

78. Chesterton, *St. Thomas Aquinas*, 109–10. One of the great twentieth-century examples of the mixed life is narrated in Spink, *Mother Theresa*.

spiritualities of love (as in Romanticism),[79] and tendencies that reinforce a religion of selfish emotional consumption and narcissism. Indeed, *eros* is a powerful Need-love rather than a pure Gift-love, to use the words of Lewis. Though it promises self-sacrifice, these boasts are also made in a desire for possession. *Eros* can also become "acquisitive and self-centered, driven more by our needs and pleasures than by the object we seek,"[80] and this is true of the *eros* that draws the soul to desire God.

As Lewis says regarding the human love of *eros*, it does not last, and it is dangerous to desire or expect it to. Similarly, experiences of spiritual highs in intimacy with God cannot be relied upon for the long walk of the Christian life. As Chris Armstrong says,

> Wise teachers of the spiritual life remind us of something we (especially Protestant evangelicals) seem often to forget: our lives as Christians are not all about single, life-changing crisis experiences. The revivalistic image of sawdust-trail conversions and emotional "altar calls" may lead some modern Christians to seek a sudden, emotional experience as the solution to their ills, but that's not how it works.[81]

Just as in marriage, a husband and wife cannot rely upon initial infatuation or strong feelings as the basis for their devotion to one another and the covenant vows they made to one another for a lifetime. It would not be right for a husband or wife to withhold love toward their spouse because at that moment they don't *feel* like it any more than as if Christians are only called to practice love toward God and others only when they *feel* like it.[82] Imagine a soldier, police officer, or first responder's love and service to country and community relying on personal feelings in the moment. Even as strong a mystic as Teresa of Avila recognized that spiritual revelations and visions are always to be tested whether they come from God rather

---

79. Rousseau stated that even if God does not objectively exist, it is better to believe and live as if he does for the sake of morality and especially happiness, a "consoling illusion." Maritain, *Three Reformers*, 125.

80. Wilken, *Early Christian Thought*, 301.

81. Armstrong, *Medieval Wisdom*, 222.

82. See also Lewis, *Pilgrim's Regress*, 163. The strength of initial passion and feelings may have led to the declaring of promises, but the promises are to be kept by principle and habit as the "feelings come and go." See Lewis's own discussion on "being in love" and the covenant of marriage in Lewis, *Mere Christianity*, in *Signature Classics*, 92–95. Although in neither chapter does Lewis identify this specifically with *eros*, see also his comments on the unreliable role of feelings in loving God, 111.

than as deceptions of Satan or one's own imagination. The heights of true mystical embrace are also not the sole ends of this life, "continuous absorption" is not possible or desirable now, and true experiences result in greater humility in helping and serving the benefit of others: "God's blessing leaves exalted desires inside the soul, which cause her to live righteously and give generously to others.... And even when the flames in the soul have cooled, her inclination to help others remains."[83] The tension of perfectly balancing and synthesizing the contemplative life and the active life for every human—other than the Son of God—was recognized by Richard Rolle as well: "If any man could achieve both lives at once, the contemplative and the active, and sustain and fulfil them, he would be great indeed. He would maintain a ministry with his body, and at the same time experience within himself the song of heaven, absorbed in melody and the joy of everlasting love."[84]

This does not mean that Christians should never desire experiences of delight in communion with God or that God is pleased only by duty that is only ever compulsory, but he also knows sinners well enough than to expect or demand unending heights of emotional enthusiasm. There is always the danger, too, as Lewis describes, that enjoyment of the gifts of God will cause people to demand selfishly from the Giver an "encore!"[85] As much as it seems glorifying to God to desire experiences of joyful union with him in contemplative prayer and worship, this can also easily slip into becoming more about what contemplative prayer and worship does to invoke delightful feelings, thereby subtly prayer and worship are manipulated *incurvatus in se*, using relationship with God ultimately as a means to self-centered ends: "emotions that are whipped up, self-centered, spiritually and morally useless."[86]

In Matt 25:31–46, Jesus does not say that the "sheep" and "goats" will be ultimately judged by the heights of their emotional enthusiasm or spiritual authenticity but rather how they actively treated the broken and needy among them. Spiritual highs experienced in contemplative prayer or

---

83. Teresa of Avila, *Interior Castle*, 136–37, 220–21, 226, 236–37. On the relationship of contemplative ecstasy to service, see also 142, 278–79, 288. Teresa likens the tension of the contemplative and active life to the Apostle Paul's own experience of spiritual visions, his personal wish to die and be with Christ, circumscribed only by his burden for serving others.

84. Rolle, *Fire of Love*, 112.

85. Lewis, *Letters to Malcolm*, 89–90.

86. Armstrong, *Medieval Wisdom*, 189.

passionate worship are not the warp and woof of daily Christian living and the endurance of living and serving in the messy frustrations of the world in friendship to Christ (*philia*). A commitment to holiness, compassion, and love also requires discipline, choice, and duty, with or without accompanying emotions, which can also be nurtured and sustained over the long term through formation in liturgical *storge*.

4

Agape
Loving God "Unconditionally" through Pain

IN HIS FINAL CHAPTER on charity (*agape*), Lewis likens human loves to tending a garden. They "are not self-sufficient." They must be cultivated by something greater for them to flourish in all the full splendor for which they were designed. In other words, human loves find their truth, beauty, and goodness underneath the supreme love of God. It not so much that people or things be loved less,[1] but that love for God is always measurably *more* and they thereby become his "instruments" infused by divine Gift-love. Lewis argues that it is also not because loving something or someone mortal, subject to loss, inevitably brings pain—as Augustine lamented in the death of his loved ones in *Confessions*. The risk of pain is not the cause for Christians to close their hearts to others or love less—"to lock it up safe in the casket or coffin of your selfishness."[2] This goes against the very example of Christ, the Suffering Servant, who was hurt precisely in his love toward enemies and friends. "To love at all is to be vulnerable," says Lewis. It is also ultimately not a matter of requiring a *feeling* of love stronger for something or someone more than God. Ultimately, when it comes to a rivalry between human loves and love of God, what will a Christian *choose* regardless of feeling? Who or what claims the *will*?[3]

---

1. Kierkegaard, *Fear and Trembling*, 101–2.
2. Lewis, *Four Loves*, 120–21.
3. Lewis, *Four Loves*, 122–24, 133–34. "That all human loves become Christian only

Lewis returns to his earlier distinction between Gift-love and Need-love. When it comes to relating human loves to love of God, Lewis begins not with "mysticism, with the creature's love for God," but with the eternal God before time who is pure Gift-love and in whom there is no Need-love, even foreseeing his own rejection in Jesus Christ by the very ones he freely created in love. "God, who needs nothing, loves into existence wholly superfluous creatures in order that He may love and perfect them." God has bestowed resemblances of his Gift-love in the natural human loves, such as in the affection of mothers for their children. He also created humans with the ability to offer themselves in Gift-love to God, including through his presence "hidden" in the needs of the neighbor. Divine Gift-love, however, offers something unique in that it also loves those who in and of themselves *have nothing to attract love or desire*, especially due to sin. To be loved by grace with *agape*, whether by God or by another person, is to be loved not for "cleverness, beauty, generosity, fairness, or usefulness." It is to be loved *as unlovable*.[4]

A disciple of Christ, in imitation of God's love, foregoes the option of self-preservation and the keeping of his or heart protected and "intact":

> The only place outside Heaven where you can be perfectly safe from all the dangers and perturbations of love is Hell. Christ did not teach and suffer that we might become, even in the natural loves, more careful of our own happiness. We shall draw nearer to God, not by trying to avoid the sufferings inherent in all loves, but by accepting them and offering them to Him; throwing away all defensive armor. If our hearts need to be broken, and if He chooses this as the way in which they should break, so be it.[5]

Some might consider Lewis's wording a bit strong here, given that it seems to encourage the allowance and endurance of abuse, rather than allowing for times where a situation of harm requires legitimate escape or reporting. However, weighed with wisdom, there is also a sense in which disciples of Christ are to love as he loved, to endure grief as a reality of loving a fallen world mercifully in likeness to God. Attempts to avoid *every* possible pain and hurt that come with extending oneself to others in generous love is

---

when the little rivulets of our many affections, desires, passions, and utopias converge into the burning torrent of the love of God." Leiva-Merikakis, *Love's Sacred Order*, 18–19, 27.

4. Lewis, *Four Loves*, 126–29.
5. Lewis, *Four Loves*, 120–21.

Agape

contrary to the love of God in Christ. In fact, even before God created the world, says Lewis, he already foresaw the "buzzing cloud of flies about the cross, the flayed back pressed against the uneven stake, the nails driving through the mesial nerves. If I may dare the biological image, God is a 'host' who deliberately creates His own parasites: causes us to be that we may exploit and 'take advantage of Him. Herein is love.'"[6] What Jesus does warn against most is in allowing other loves to come between or hinder love for him and by extension God the Father.

While *storge*, *philia*, and *eros* are naturally attainable human loves without grace, *agape* sanctifies and perfects them, making it the only love that is necessarily also divine. It is the most unnatural or unhuman because it loves even when there is no reciprocation or benefit. In fact, it loves even in the face of hate and evil. *Agape* is the one love that is beyond fallen human capacity and that God himself *must* enable:

> You have heard that it was said, "Love your neighbor and hate your enemy." But I tell you, love your enemies and pray for those who persecute you, that you may be children of your Father in heaven. He causes his sun to rise on the evil and the good, and sends rain on the righteous and the unrighteous. If you love those who love you, what reward will you get? Are not even the tax collectors doing that? And if you greet only your own people, what are you doing more than others? Do not even pagans do that? Be perfect, therefore, as your heavenly Father is perfect. (Matt 5:43–48)

As with a marriage, sometimes the emotional desire for union (*eros*) is not there. Sometimes the friendship (*philia*) is harmed when there is disunity of value or perspective. Affection (*storge*) may be present, but it can often be taken for granted and not fully appreciated until a major change or loss of the relationship occurs. This is where *agape* would enter. It is not based on any delightful quality that compels desire for union (*eros*), the sharing of a common vision or quest (*philia*), or the familiar bond of affection (*storge*). It is a love of *pure choice*, what might be called duty or what Kant defined as the deontological ethic.[7] It is a determination to do what is right or good without thought of consequence, of personal advantage or disadvantage. It is also the Gift-love that is most vulnerable to pain. It is the love that gives and gives when there is nothing lovable or worthy in what is loved. *Agape* is the love that is truly the most selfless.

---

6. Lewis, *Four Loves*, 127.
7. Boyd and Thorsen, *Christian Ethics*, 5, 103–13.

Unlike humanity, only God exists as pure "Gift-love." He needs nothing from us although he is perfectly worthy of all things. There is nothing that humans could ever do to attract or return the gift of divine compassion and mercy toward sinners. Yet, there is a sense in which the Christian can love God with a Gift-love:

> Finally, by a high paradox, God enables men to have a Gift-love toward Himself. There is of course a sense in which no one can give to God anything which is not already His; and if it is already His, what have you given? But since it is only too obvious that we can withhold ourselves, our wills and hearts, from God, we can, in that sense, also give them. What is His by right and would not exist for a moment if it ceased to be His, He has nevertheless made ours in such a way that we can freely give back to Him.[8]

Lewis concludes *The Four Loves* by exploring the possibility of a disinterested love toward God. It is a delighting awe in God and his beauty regardless of self. This is pure "supernatural Appreciative love," which Lewis says God can "awaken in man." This love delights in a thing on its own pure merit even if not needed or benefited from, such as admiring water even when not feeling thirsty. In the opening pages of *The Four Loves*, Lewis is skeptical that creatures defined by needs can ever love God so disinterestedly: "Exalted souls may tell us of a reach beyond [Need-love]" for God, but it would be delusional to think that such "heights" of this godlike form of Gift-love can be *sustained* as if we could expect to "live on them." Later, Lewis says that a "supernatural Appreciative love" for God

> of all gifts is the most to be desired. Here, not in our natural loves, nor even in ethics, lies the true center of all human and angelic life. God knows, not I, whether I have ever tasted this love. Perhaps I have only imagined the tasting. Those like myself whose imagination far exceeds their obedience are subject to a just penalty; we easily imagine conditions far higher than any we have really achieved.[9]

Agape: Loving God without Condition

The Cistercian monk and theologian Bernard of Clairvaux in the Middle Ages spoke of "loving God for His own sake," which is greater than to love

---

8. Lewis, *Four Loves*, 128–29.
9. Lewis, *Four Loves*, 3–4, 140.

God for *the self's sake*. The latter is not to be rejected as a valid love, as Jesus said that whoever is forgiven little loves little (Luke 7:47), and the higher love cannot be reached for Bernard except through the lower (in Lewis's terms, Need-love). Yet the more God is known through his spiritual and earthly gifts, the more, Bernard says, hearts may ascend to a love of God as he simply is, and not just by the benefits he gives: "He who trusts in the Lord not because he is good to him but simply because he is good truly loves God for God's sake and not for his own. He of whom it is said, 'He will praise you when you do him favors' (Ps 48:19), does not love in this way."[10] In *The Great Divorce*, there is a way spoken of in "treating God only as a means.... But the whole thickening treatment consists of learning to want God for his own sake."[11]

There are many passages throughout Scripture that affirm a love of God that is faithful even through great loss and suffering. Israel was led to hunger in the wilderness so that their love of God could be tested as greater than their desperation for physical bread (Deut 8:2–3). Jesus, first in his own wilderness temptation (Matt 4:1–11; Luke 4:1–13) and then culminating years later in submission to the Father's will before the cross in a period of tremendous suffering and agony in Gethsemane (Matt 26:39), was qualified to be the perfectly righteous High Priest and Mediator between God and humanity (Heb 5:7–9). The New Testament takes for granted the suffering of God's elect, that it is not something to be spurned, but something to be embraced in the joy that Christians are becoming more like their Savior and Lord—the end of salvation (Rom 8:28–29; Jas 1:2–3; 1 Pet 1:6–9). Jesus himself said that suffering can be a blessing deserving of great reward when endured patiently and faithfully (Matt 5:10–12).

Suffering in Ancient and Medieval Catholicism

Early Christians knew much about suffering as their devotion to Christ was often met with Roman government oppression, social hatred, brutal torture and execution, and public ridicule in the spectacle of the Roman theater. (It is important to acknowledge that violent persecution is still experienced by millions of Christians today in regions of Africa, the Middle East, and Asia.) The moving testimony of the martyr Perpetua in the third century is of a woman having to let go of familial bonds to her pagan father and

---

10. Bernard, "On Loving God," in *Selected Works*, 174–75, 194.
11. Lewis, *Great Divorce*, in *Signature Classics*, 518.

separation from her own infant child to be willingly subjected for the sake of Christ to mockery and death in the form of Roman public entertainment.[12]

While the cessation of persecution with Roman emperor Constantine in the early fourth century brought new opportunities for Christians to experience a greater abundance of worldly peace and prosperity, a group of zealous-minded individuals were inspired to follow in the footsteps of the holy virtue of the ancient martyrs by adopting a life of *self-inflicted* suffering and martyrdom. The desert dwellers chose a life withdrawn from the city and the allurements of traditional power, prestige, and wealth, now made available to a greater number of church members of the high classes under Christianity's new imperial popularity, pomp, and patronage.

Benedict of Nursia's sixth-century hilltop community of Monte Cassino, apart from the vows foregoing personal wealth, ambitious independence, and sexual delights, taught the brothers that the way to ascend to God is opposite the path of worldly glory, by humility and submission. This involved the acceptance not only of the hardships that come with vowing to live in a community life devoted to uprooting selflessness in monastic discipline, but in the "fourth step of humility." This is the test of persevering obedience "under difficult, unfavorable, or even unjust conditions" in sacred conformity to the life of their Lord.[13]

In modern society, where every Epicurean effort is made to avoid pain and know pleasure, the choice of ancient and medieval ascetics and mystics in favor of discipline, fasting, and self-restraint of creaturely comforts and pleasures certainly sounds harsh and downright strange. Who would *choose* to withhold from the self all the pleasures at one's disposal or to endure suffering and pain with joy when there are so many good things in this life to be experienced and enjoyed? Only those who can see in pain and suffering the means to a greater, eternal end than fleeting satisfactions, just as Screwtape warns Wormwood that the "Enemy" (God) gains greater possession of a soul through "troughs even more than on the peaks; some of his special favorites have gone through longer and deeper troughs than anyone else."[14]

For ancient and medieval ascetics like Augustine, Benedict, or Francis of Assisi, it was not a manner of despising the good, created world that God had made, like heretical dualist Manichaeans from Persia or the Cathars

---

12. Litfin, "Perpetua," in *Know the Church Fathers*, 119–40.
13. Benedict, *Rule of Saint Benedict*, 18.
14. Lewis, *Screwtape Letters*, in *Signature Classics*, 207.

of medieval France, but putting to death the part of human nature that so weakly clamors and attaches itself to the seduction of loving creaturely idols more than God, that irrationally prefers temporal and fleeting pleasures to the eternal and permanent prize won painfully by self-restraint and virtue enabled by the grace of God. As Chesterton astutely observed, it was the same Francis who sang the praises of creation who paradoxically chose to suffer a life of humble poverty rather than indulgence.[15]

In the medieval Catholic ascetic tradition, to see God necessitates that one become more like God who is other than creation. This is why souls ascending toward God in heavenly paradise in Dante's *Purgatorio* receive their painful discipline with desire and gladness (unlike souls in hell who can only chaff in despair at their permanent situation), because they know their suffering is purging the remnants of self-love and making their souls fit to behold and enjoy the freedom of the perfection of heaven and the pure vision of God.[16] Like recognizes and affirms like. To see and enjoy a room filled with bright light, the eyes accustomed to darkness must be adjusted to the light. If the path to union with God is a movement from self-love to greater self-denial, medievals understood that this requires pain in the process, because godliness runs contrary to the aspirations of fallen human nature. If loving God more means loving oneself less, how can this happen without some pain, especially before having acquired a disposition and habit toward the good—much like the pain experienced when dilated pupils are first inundated with a bright light?

So far, this chapter has focused on sufferings for being a Christian or the choosing of ascetic discipline for the cultivation of virtue in preparation for heaven, but the Old Testament figure of Job loomed as a prime example for early and medieval Christians of the struggle to love God in hardships that are unexplained and not chosen—a form of testing that reveals inward spiritual wealth and that (and in Job's particular case) produces an even greater temporal reward. John Chrysostom and Pope Gregory the Great similarly viewed Job as the archetypal godly sufferer, a man who could literally lose everything except his life in a single day and yet, with no clear cause for God's allowance of pain, struggled to choose faith and keep his favor with God. In the wake of the surprising and devastating sack of Rome by tribal invaders in AD 410, Augustine reminded Christians belonging to the heavenly City of God that they are not immune to the vicissitudes of

---

15. Chesterton, *St. Thomas Aquinas*, 51, 111.
16. Dante, *Purgatorio*.

living in the fallen earthly City of Man: war, poverty, hunger, disease, and ultimately death affect everyone. But for the true Christian and lover of God, he or she endures earthly losses with patience and hope in an eternal blessedness that cannot be spoiled or destroyed.[17]

Although not using explicitly Christian language, Boethius's *Consolation of Philosophy* (a favorite of Lewis) describes in semi-autobiography the vexation of the sixth-century author in his fall from the king's grace in Ostrogothic-ruled Italy. In conversation with Philosophy personified, Boethius is encouraged to think less on the unpredictable character of Fortune (or rather its predictability of change, "her true nature") and to prize his "true good" over the evanescent happiness of worldly fame, wealth, and power. Indeed, in response to the question, What profit is there in virtue when suffering is unavoidable and the wicked seem to flourish the most (Ps 75)? an answer is given by Philosophy that

> good fortune always seems to bring happiness, but deceives you with her smiles . . . but bad fortune enlightens. With her display of specious riches good fortune enslaves the minds of those who enjoy her, while bad fortune gives men release through the recognition of how fragile a thing happiness is.[18]

Not only that, but the rise of prosperity is often accompanied by the fall of virtue, and in the end, it is the condition of the soul toward God that endures: "Good fortune lures men away from the path of true good, but adverse fortune frequently draws men back to their true good like a shepherdess with her crook." And what is that "true and perfect good"? "Disperse the clouds of earthly matter's cloying weight," sings Philosophy in ode to Her eternal God, "Shine in all Thy glory; for Thou art rest and peace, To those who worship Thee; to see Thee is our end, Who art our source and maker, lord and path and goal."[19]

This was Paul's spiritual secret expressed in his prison letter to the Philippians: "I know what it is to be in need, and I know what it is to have plenty. I have learned the secret of being content in any and every situation, whether well fed or hungry, whether living in plenty or in want. I can do all this through him who gives me strength" (Phil 4:11–13). This theme of living a serene and steady existence amidst the changing circumstances of human life was praised in the theology of ancient Hebrew wisdom literature

---

17. Walsh and Walsh, *Divine Providence and Human Suffering*, 111–14, 120–26.
18. Boethius, *Consolation of Philosophy*, 55, 76.
19. Boethius, *Consolation of Philosophy*, 96–98.

as well as Neo-Platonic and Stoic philosophy, and the doxological virtue of surrendering to the mysteries of Providence is echoed later by Protestant Reformers such as John Calvin (whose first work was a commentary on the Roman philosopher Seneca).

Affliction and Protestant Theology

Medievals idealized loving God purely without self-interest, as well as the related emphasis placed on loving God through suffering and pain. This partly explains the repressive motivation to voluntary suffering—sometimes to extreme lengths—in the ancient and medieval monastic movements. It also explains some of the physical and psychological burden that nearly broke Luther's mind in the monastery. The Protestant doctrine of justification and inheritance of eternal life by faith alone in the complete righteousness of Christ removed suffering as a penitential and purgatorial work of satisfaction—certainly as if suffering itself was meritorious—but it also mitigated heaven as the reward of inner moral perfection acquired through suffering. Perhaps if there is any distortion of *agape*, it is in a desire for pain and harm that border on the masochistic.

The early Protestant Reformers rejected the reality and the redemptive use of postmortem purgatory, lacking a strong biblical basis, and they closed the monastic schools of asceticism and the chantry chapel Masses that encouraged belief in it. Yet they did not negate the expectation of suffering or its sanctifying work in *this life* for the Christian justified by faith alone. In fact, contrary to later extreme Pentecostal emphases on this-worldly prosperity as a promise of the gospel and Christ's victory over the forces of evil, Protestants from Luther on continued to view suffering as possessing an expected and needful role in the life of the believer. Along with faith and the Holy Spirit (through the ministry of word and sacrament), suffering serves in disciplining and mortifying the Christian's old nature, keeps the sufferer on his knees before God in humble need, and maintains the soul's orientation toward the future glory and righteousness that awaits in heaven for the justified. Although Christians "see from our daily experience in life that we are subjected to all kinds of things, suffer many things, even die," Luther says the Christian is lord over suffering and death through the enduring and strengthening of faith in the eternal triumph of Christ.[20]

20. Luther, *Freedom of a Christian*, 505.

Within the heritage of Protestant Christianity, few provided more extensive pastoral counsel for those experiencing unwanted afflictions than the English Puritans. Thomas Watson, in his book originally entitled *Divine Cordial* (1663) and based on Rom 8:28,[21] lists ten reasons from Scripture that suffering as a lover of God leads to good. Affliction is a furnace in which the soul rises from earthly attachments to its true resting place in God and in conformity to the image of the suffering Christ: "Was His head crowned with thorns, and do we think to be crowned with roses? It is good to be like Christ, though it be by sufferings."[22] For Watson as well as for Lewis, affliction in the hand of God comes from a love that transcends a grandfatherly, sentimental kindness and wants to awaken the Christian soul to what is most pleasing to God and best for the spiritual health of the soul made for eternity. That God uses affliction to chisel sinful human beings into splendorous and holy works of doxological art comes from the Divine Artist having a greater love, not less, toward his works.[23]

In the wake of world catastrophes in the twentieth century, modern Protestant and Catholic theologies developed a new emphasis on the sympathy of God for human suffering, experienced in God's love being rejected and in the forsakenness of the Son on the cross by the Father, thus interpreting God less as a sovereign above and more as an immanent sufferer with mankind in history. Contrary to ancient Platonic and Aristotelian metaphysics, that the supreme deity is impassive and unaffected (*apatheia*) by history and human suffering (unlike the mythical gods of Mount Olympus), Jürgen Moltmann and others, including German Lutheran Dietrich Bonhoeffer and Japanese theologians Kazoh Kitamori and Kosuke Koyama, have focused on the incarnation and cross of Christ as revealing the mystery of pain and suffering (*pathos*) in the nature of God with and for the world.[24] That God somehow understands what it is to suffer might offer a comforting word, but without the promise that God can and also will in his sovereign love redeem the pain for the triumph of ultimate good is to leave the sufferer without a basis for hope.

---

21. Watson, *All Things for Good*.

22. Watson, *All Things for Good*, 27–32.

23. Lewis, *Problem of Pain*, 30–36.

24. Moltmann, *Crucified God*, 267–78; Bauckham, "Only the Suffering God"; Parratt, *Third World Theologies*, 90–93.

Loving God with *Agape*: "Judge Not the Lord"

It might be going out on limb to suggest that as with the other three loves, God can be loved with charity (*agape*), or unconditionally, especially through pain. God is without sin, yet who has not felt at times that it is hard to love God, especially when facing a particular suffering—like Job—without a clear reason? What Christian has not been tempted to be angry with God, to put him on trial, accuse him of injustice, and maybe even consider him to be acting as an enemy rather than a loving Father?

Lewis experienced exactly this upon the death of his wife, Joy, in 1960, evoking Lewis's raw and originally pseudonymous work, *A Grief Observed*. He describes coming to God in his agony and finding the door slammed shut and double-bolted. Lewis felt himself tested like Christians of times past. How could they have accepted his will while feeling such torture of the soul inside? Was their act to love God just that? An act? Lewis expresses less a temptation to atheism than to thinking "dreadful things" about the God who is there: "So this is what God's really like?" A "Cosmic Sadist?" Lewis admits that sometimes it is "hard not to say, 'God forgive God.'" His conclusion is choosing to believe that, if God is good, then pain can serve a good in his hands—one of which is to reveal that a temple of faith was actually a "house of cards." Another is that Christians come to terms not with their "idea of God, but God," and with God as goal not "a road" (the ends not a means).[25]

Years before, in *The Problem of Pain*, Lewis says learning to love God for his own sake irrespective of feeling will be accompanied by some pain, because only a choice made "from the pure will to obey, in the absence, or in the teeth, of inclination" is done against self-regard.[26] One might also say that this kind of love requires the most faith. This is the love of the *will*, the *choosing* to deny what the self feels it wants, which makes it the most difficult and unachievable in natural human strength. The particular reason for the suffering may lack clear meaning, but the will chooses to love God even when the meaning of his working may be mysterious and does not, as Niebuhr says, "conform fully to the patterns of meaning which human beings are able to construct." Yet the alternative, as accepted by the modern

---

25. Lewis, *Grief Observed*, in *Signature Classics*, 658–59, 668, 673–75, 684–85.
26. Lewis, *Problem of Pain*, 87.

nihilists, is "the despairing conclusion that there is no meaning in the total historical enterprise," especially in the face of universal death.[27]

As Lewis concludes in *The Four Loves*, "'Is it easy to love God?' asks an old author. It is easy for those who do it."[28] *Eros* may boast the will to abandon the good of the self for the sake of a beloved, but it is *agape* that endures when *eros* fades and when the unbearable pain and loss tempt the will to stray. Perhaps loving God as *agape*—for himself, regardless of his benefits, and even through sufferings—is of all the loves the one love of God that most requires the help of his divine grace and power.

To trust God is to love him with charity even when he seems to hide behind "a frowning providence," in the words of the British poet and hymn writer William Cowper ("God Moves in a Mysterious Way," 1774): "Judge not the Lord by feeble sense, but trust him for his grace; behind a frowning providence, he hides a smiling face. His purposes will ripen fast, unfolding every hour; the bud may have a bitter taste, but sweet will be the flower."[29] It is to choose to say with Job, "Naked came I out of my mother's womb, and naked shall I return thither: the Lord gave, and the Lord hath taken away; blessed be the name of the Lord. . . . Though He slay me, yet will I trust Him" (Job 1:21; 13:15 KJV). It is to obey even when what is most cherished is mysteriously demanded, as in the story of Abraham and Isaac (Gen 22:1–19). "Only in the moment when his act is in contradiction with his feeling, only then does he sacrifice Isaac," says Kierkegaard.[30] It is a love that says:

> Though the fig tree does not bud
> and there are no grapes on the vines,
> though the olive crop fails
> and the fields produce no food,
> though there are no sheep in the pen
> and no cattle in the stalls,
> yet I will rejoice in the Lord,
> I will be joyful in God my Savior. (Hab 3:17–18)

---

27. Niebuhr, *Faith and History*, 132.
28. Lewis, *Four Loves*, 140.
29. Cowper, "God Moves," 261.
30. Kierkegaard, *Fear and Trembling*, 101–2.

5

Fractured Loves and the Secular Age

THE FOUR LOVES—*STORGE*, *PHILIA*, *eros*, and *agape*—are perfectly integrated in the person and life of Jesus Christ. He criticized the Jewish leaders for their moral hypocrisy, but he continued to love the Father in *storge*, honoring him through liturgies of worship in synagogue and temple. The mission of Jesus was in perfect union with the will of the Father (*philia*) in an active ministry of truth telling, miracles of compassion, and generous self-sacrifice. As active as Jesus was, he also desired personal union with the Father in private prayer (*eros*). Lastly, he loved the Father to the point of drinking the dreaded, bitter cup by unjustly enduring the forsaken, crushing blow of justice on behalf of sinners (*agape*).

Each love brings something to the table and at the same time checks extremes that would diminish and distort the Christian love of God. *Storge* unites Christians collectively and publicly in expressing affectionate devotion to God through liturgical worship, which involves rituals centered on word and sacrament that span time and space to form (and reform) Christians in mind and body. *Philia* is the love of God that expresses friendship with Christ in the world, sharing in his vision of the kingdom of God, as well as following him in his peaceable *way* of growing the kingdom until he returns. *Eros* expresses the desire of individuals to know God personally and to experience union with his eternal, divine life in such a way that brings true and holy feelings of joy, peace, and love. *Agape* is the choice of loving God even amid unexplained sufferings, when God feels distant, or it feels difficult to love God through pain and afflictions. Examples of these four loves were illustrated in the broad history of Christianity.

Each love of God offers its own unique contribution to the whole as well as its own problems when untethered from the others and given excess. As was demonstrated by a look at various, diverse movements in the unfolding of historical Christianity in Catholic, Orthodox, and Protestant traditions, the one love of God often became many, fractured rather than whole, competing rather than complimentary. Though not always severed in every case, Christian history is replete with movements of correction and overcorrection leading to imbalance,[1] and in this case the full love of God was often fractured and diminished, as was the total body of Christ sent "into the world" but "not of the world" (John 17:14–19).

This problem was not isolated to one tradition but is truly ecumenical. One goal of this book, by surveying the broad, "catholic" history of Christianity was to stimulate a conversation among Christians regarding the benefits and the continuing problems associated with each form of loving God. Falling to extremes is naturally human and easier. To approach the center and to balance tension might be more challenging but mediating between either/or in favor of both/and oftentimes brings us much closer to the truth. As the seventeenth-century French Catholic Blaise Pascal wisely urged, greatness is not found in extremes but by "touching both at once and occupying all the spaces in between."[2]

Major movements that shifted historical Christianity, among other social, cultural, theological, economic, and political factors, could be additionally seen as the fracturing of the four loves (and this is especially true for the already splintering nature of Protestantism). Loving God through *storge* to the diminishing of *eros* and *philia* prompted movements of reformation and pietist revival against church ritualism in the fifteenth and sixteenth centuries. Likewise, efforts to love God through *eros* and *agape* in monasticism and late medieval Catholic mysticism was challenged by Protestant theologies of salvation by faith and the sanctity of all callings contributing to human prosperity in this world—including diverting religiously-inspired devotion towards the needs of the *living* neighbor (*philia*).

Divisions and wars in Europe between Protestants and Catholics and within Protestantism over doctrinal beliefs and *storge*, and schisms created

---

1. Cameron, *Interpreting Christian History*, 102, 229–40.
2. Pascal, *Pensées*, 243 (no. 353). The devil corrupts by offering extremes. Lewis, *Screwtape Letters*, in *Signature Classics*, 183.

Fractured Loves and the Secular Age

by dissenting groups devoted to radical *eros*, provoked the new search of Enlightenment rational philosophy for universal religious morality while natural law and science transformed the way educated people thought about God, humanity, and the world. This eventually led to redefining religion by severing dependence upon the empowering life and wisdom of God and loosening ethics (*philia*) from the grace of supernatural sanctification in Christ (*storge* and *eros*). This is what Catholic philosopher Jacques Maritain describes as the "naturalization of Christianity," or the efforts to "keep the human aspirations of Christianity but do away with Christ."[3]

The Christian love of God as *eros* emphasized among Catholic mystics, Protestant Pietists, charismatics, and Pentecostals, unbalanced by an equal emphasis on *philia* and *storge* concentrated Christian desire on individual feelings and heights of emotional, spiritual experiences through contemplation, worship, or the miraculous. This emphasis on personal union with God taken to excess fostered subjective, spiritual self-absorption, which in some ways mirrored the vague longing of nineteenth-century Romantics for a personal feeling of mystical oneness with God (or nature or beauty). It is no surprise that, without caution, this has a potential to reduce the communal significance of liturgical worship and (or) distract from the active life of selfless service and commitment to human needs.

Although there are exceptions, historical Christianity generally shows a challenge in maintaining a perfect blending and union of these loves of God. Yet the loves together centripetally restrain the others from veering off independently on their own into excess and corruption. A proper stress on *philia* and *storge* can hold *eros* back from extreme emotionalism, individualism, and social inactivity. *Eros* and *philia* can preserve *storge* from becoming complacent ritualism, and *eros* and *storge* can prevent the movement toward self-righteous, secular philosophical moralism.

---

3. "Is not all this the whole essence of the Revolution?" Maritain, *Three Reformers*, 122–23.

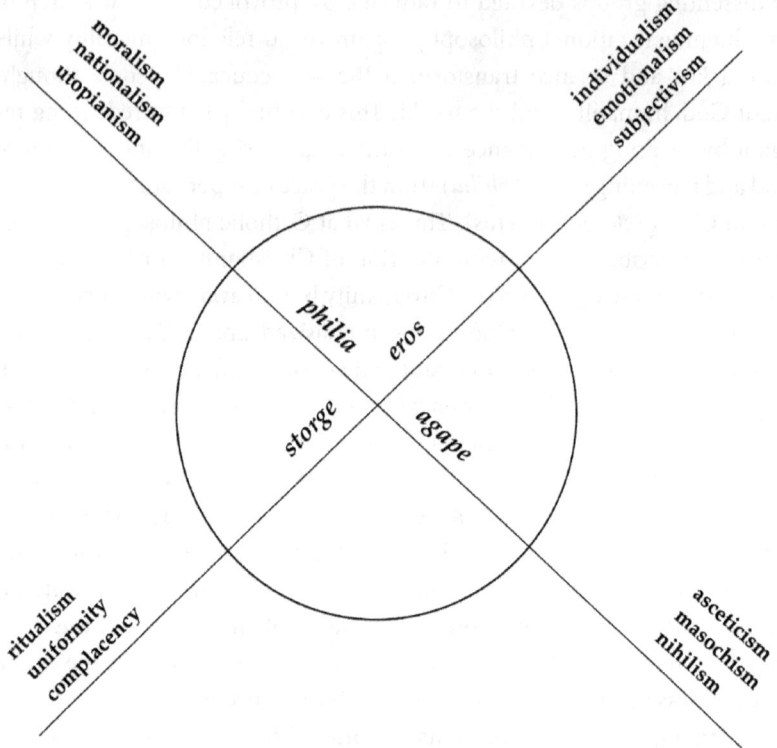

Along with other emerging realities that shaped the modern world—urbanization, democracy, scientific knowledge, commercial industry, and technology—could it be said that it was the fracturing of these four loves in Christian history that even contributed something to the rise of the secular worldview option in the eighteenth and nineteenth centuries? In focusing excessively on one of these loves, the Christian love of God was deformed, and while the perfection of these loves is found in their integration, when separated, they became half-truths in conflict with each other. That conflict and separation have contributed to many of the problems that are facing the modern, secular age. If this is true, what hope might the balanced integration of the four loves have for Christians in not only resisting a reduced and diminished love of God but also joining a growing chorus in challenging the prevailing narrative that drives much of the modern secular myth and confidence in human progress?[4]

4. E.g., Dreher, *Benedict Option*.

Fractured Loves and the Secular Age

The Myth of Modern Progress and the New Humanity

Modern secular humanism emerged in the eighteenth and nineteenth centuries in the form of an egoistic denial of God (or the human need of God so far understood). In forsaking traditional religion in the practices of contemplative prayer, liturgical worship, and the authority of the Bible, a new generation of thinkers boasted pretentiously in humanity's ability—now unrestrained—to master nature and perfect the world through advances in scientific knowledge, moral philosophy, political policy, and united willpower. This could be said to be a modern collective form of the ancient heresy of Pelagianism,[5] not defined as individual salvation or the power of human righteousness to enter a heavenly realm beyond space-time, but as modern humanity's collective confidence that it possessed the intellectual and moral resources *to reopen Eden and build paradise on earth.*

The character Ransom, in Lewis's *That Hideous Strength* (1945), encounters such scientific ambition, moral self-righteousness, and seduction of increasing power over nature at the militant organization N.I.C.E.:

> "Does it follow that because there was no God in the past that there will be no God also in the future? . . . Don't you see . . . that we are offering you the unspeakable glory of being present at the creation of God Almighty. Here, in this house, you shall meet the first sketch of the real God. It is a man—or a being made by man—who will finally ascend the throne of the universe. And rule forever." . . . There was now at last a real chance for fallen Man to shake off that limitation of his powers which mercy had imposed upon him as a protection from the full results of the fall. If this succeeded, Hell itself would be at last incarnate.[6]

In a separate essay by Lewis, he likewise opines, "I dread government in the name of science. That is how tyrannies come in. . . . The question about progress has become the question whether we can discover any way of submitting to the world-wide paternalism of a technocracy without losing

---

5. Pelagius was a fifth-century monk who taught that humans have the natural will to turn from sin and obey the Law of God to earn personal salvation. His ideas were refuted by Augustine, who insisted on the need for the inward help of God's grace and Holy Spirit in the conversion and sanctification of the sinner: "Give what you command, and command what you will." Augustine, *Confessions*, 240 (bk. 10, ch. 31). Augustine's interpretation of Phil 2:12–13 was a key text in his anti-Pelagian writings.

6. Lewis, *That Hideous Strength*, 176, 200.

all personal privacy and independence."[7] Orwell's *1984* comes to mind, as well as Huxley's *Brave New World*. The union of government and biological science in the efforts to create a pure race and superior society motivated Himmler's racial eugenic strategies in Nazi Germany.[8]

The horrific tragedies of the twentieth century, which Lewis lived through in two world wars, were the fruits of unrestrained human pretension that began with the optimism of the Enlightenment. Immanuel Kant coined the word "Enlightenment" (*Aufklärung*) to describe the dawning of a new age of rational thought in the eighteenth century. Kant affirmed the individual liberation and autonomy to think and act morally on the basis of reason in revolt against blind faith and dependency on claims of spiritual revelation from episcopal or biblical authorities—which religious war had proved were sources of knowledge devoid of human consensus.[9] Liberation from monarchial and aristocratic power as well as their historical alignment with the church led to its most radical eighteenth-century form during the French Revolution in a ceremony devoted to enshrining the goddess of reason in Notre Dame Cathedral in 1793.[10] This ritual could be viewed as a secular or pagan *storge* oriented toward the realization of a new secular vision or mission of a Christ-less, humanist *philia*.

Modernity would thus be defined by an intellectual and moral optimism that natural humanity, without the help of the special revelation or redemptive grace of God in Christ, can approach utopia on earth through its own terrestrial resources—through more scientific advances, greater technological and machine efficiency, and advances in education and political legislation. While the enlightenment "of the few" became the secularization "of the many" nearer the twentieth century,[11] Christianity was viewed by elites in the eighteenth and nineteenth centuries as either needing a significant theological renovation (i.e., Protestant liberalism) or its more complete secular marginalization in the march toward human progress and world change. For the atheists of the new revolution, "the unity of the world, which was not achieved with [belief in] God, will henceforth

---

7. Lewis, "Is Progress Possible?," in *God in the Dock*, 315–16.
8. Kater, *Hitler Youth*, 94–112.
9. Kant, "Answer to the Question," 33–46.
10. "Temple of Reason," 168–73; Taylor, *Secular Age*, 222–24. On the French Revolution, see also McLeod, *Religion*, 1–21; Aston, *Religion and Revolution*, 259–76.
11. Noll et al., *Turning Points*, 230. Noll quotes from Chadwick, *Secularization of the European Mind*, 5, 9; McLeod, *Secularization in Western Europe*.

be attempted in defiance of [belief in] God."[12] What H. Richard Niebuhr characterizes in liberalism as "cultural Christianity" is argued to have given birth to "movements that tended toward the extreme of self-reliant humanism, which found the doctrine of grace—and even more the reliance upon it—demeaning to man and discouraging to his will."[13] In the later Romantic defense of Milton's devil in paradise, Christianity and its historic beliefs were viewed by modern philosophers as restraining human potential. Thus, it was Christianity that needed restraining if humankind was to break free and ascend to its rightful place as lords of the world.

The German atheist Ludwig Feuerbach argued in *Essence of Christianity* (1841) that the metaphysical ideas of Christianity are not related to anything ontologically real but merely the idealized projection of what humanity collectively (i.e., the state) had the potential to become and achieve in a world without God.[14] Feuerbach influenced Marx who expressed his own criticism of religion (Christianity) as harmfully justifying oppressive structures of the wealthy in industrial capitalism. Marx believed revolution of economic circumstances and compulsion of a more just society would free people from the inhibiting illusion of Christianity.[15]

The quest of modern humanity in a collective sense, then, is to become its own god.[16] At the end of H. G. Wells's science fiction novel *The Food of the Gods* (1904), giants created by scientifically engineered food resist efforts to be controlled and praise the unquenchable thirst and fact of nature that self-conscious beings desire to move toward ever new heights of greatness (and this will not stop at conquering the inhabited earth):

> "It is in the nature of all things; it is part of space and time. To grow and still to grow; from first to last that is Being—that is the law of life.... To grow, and again to grow—to grow. To grow at last

---

12. Camus, *Rebel*, 61.

13. Niebuhr, *Christ and Culture*, 113.

14. Feuerbach, *Essence of Christianity*; Moltmann *Crucified God*, 251-52. "To recognize that there is no God, and not to recognize at the same time that you have become God, is an absurdity.... Once you recognize it, you are king, and you will not kill yourself but will live in the chiefest glory.... For three years I have been searching for the attribute of my divinity, and I have found it: the attribute of my divinity is—Self-will!" Dostoyevsky, *Demons*, 619. The character Kirillov concludes that he must prove the point by the ultimate act of self-will, suicide. On surrealism, moral nihilism, and unrestrained violence against self and society, see also Camus, *Rebel*, 92-93.

15. Janz, *World Christianity and Marxism*, 8-14.

16. Gay, *Way of the (Modern) World*, 103.

into the fellowship and understanding of God. Growing . . . Till the earth is no more than a footstool . . . Till the spirit shall have driven fear into nothingness, and spread . . .". He swung his arm heavenward: "There!"[17]

Pushing the boundaries of knowledge, power, and mortality, the end is complete freedom, self-sufficiency, and rule of the cosmos, but in a Promethean world *without God* (or dependence upon the mere *idea* of God). At the very least, it will be a world that no longer needs belief in the personal, supranatural and supraspatial, eternal God "out there" as defined by biblical theism: "We shall eventually be no more able to convince men of the existence of God 'out there' whom they must call on to order their lives than persuade them to take seriously the gods of Olympus. If Christianity is to survive, let alone to recapture the 'secular' man, there is no time to lose in detaching it from this scheme of thought."[18]

As the Devil spoke in a dream to the character Ivan Fyodorovich in Dostoyevsky's *Brothers Karamazov*, it is only a world that has repudiated God that is open for the "man-God" to appear, to replace "the former hopes of celestial pleasures" with the "vanquishing of nature . . . by his will and science."[19] Idealization of the potentiality and perfectibility of humanity by itself thereby minimizes or disavows human individual and collective propensity to sin and its absolute necessary resolution through Jesus Christ—the *only* perfect man, God incarnate.[20]

German Lutheran pastor Dietrich Bonhoeffer witnessed to his own demise the deifying of the human (and racist/nationalist) spirit in the rise of Hitler's glorious ambitions for the Nazi Reich. The new god in the "godless" modern age of the West replaced the God of Christianity with "the new human being, whether the 'factory of new humanity'" was in Nazi Germany or Communist Russia.[21] In the current era, the hope of a better world is associated with developments along a path many find promising toward

---

17. Wells, *Food of the Gods*, 637, 639. On humanity's natural ambition to expand the boundaries of human knowledge and power in conquest of outer space, see the science fiction works of Polish author Stanislaw Lem, especially *Solaris*, *His Master's Voice*, and *The Invincible*.

18. Robinson, *Honest to God*, 43. It will be interesting to see how modern physics and string theory affect the theological and scientific conversation on the existence of other spatial or dimensional realities.

19. Dostoyevsky, *Brothers Karamazov*, 829–30.

20. Machen, *Christianity and Liberalism*, 55–56, 100–102, 116–17.

21. Bonhoeffer, *Ethics*, 121–24.

a dawning age of transhumanism: gene editing, brain-computer interfaces, artificial intelligence, artificial wombs, and anti-aging technology.[22] What promises a future of greater ease, comfort, efficiency, and longevity for human life is speeding alarmingly ahead without equal concern for making people *morally* better.[23] For many who consider increasing mastery of nature not only *the* goal of humanity but an achievable one, God (or even the idea of God) will recede to irrelevancy even more in the world of tomorrow.[24] Neil Postman describes the coming of "Technopoly" as looking to "technical progress" as "humanity's supreme achievement by which our most profound dilemmas may be solved," which promises "heaven on earth through the convenience of technological progress."[25]

By making a god of science and idealizing it as the means of total mastery and manipulation of nature for human flourishing, perceived as *the* goal of human existence in modernity, it thereby corrupts the gift of human knowledge into idolatry, whose outcome is its own destruction.[26] In the words of T. S. Eliot:

> A wrong attitude toward nature implies, somewhere, a wrong attitude towards God, and that the consequence is an inevitable doom. . . . We have been accustomed to regard "progress" as always integral; and have yet to learn that it is only by an effort and a discipline, greater than society has yet seen the need of imposing upon itself, that material knowledge and power is gained without loss of spiritual knowledge and power.[27]

The ambition of humanity to master nature divorced from God without humble restraint, and the confidence it places in its own rational and scientific intelligence to exceed limits has led to the marvelous horrors of modern human creativity. Shelley captures this in her story of Dr. Victor Frankenstein, who, after scorning his laboratory experiment turned vengeful murderer beyond his control, lamented, "I conceived and executed the creation of a man. Even now I cannot recollect without passion my reveries while the work was incomplete. I trod heaven in my thoughts, now exulting

---

22. Rana and Samples, *Humans 2.0*.

23. Ellul, *Technological Society*; Gay, *Way of the (Modern) World*, 90; Postman, *Technopoly*, 42, 45.

24. Gay, *Way of the (Modern) World*, 82, 103.

25. Postman, *Technopoly*, 71, 179.

26. Gay, *Way of the (Modern) World*, 102–3.

27. Eliot, "From *The Idea of a Christian Society*," 291.

in my powers, now burning with the idea of their effects. From my infancy I was imbued with high hopes and a lofty ambition; but how I am sunk!"[28]

Freedom becomes a demon when freedom becomes a god. The promises of the industrial age of the late nineteenth-century era of "progress" met the challenge of new social tensions in overcrowded urban environments, conflict between economic classes and racial tension, pollution of the environment, degradation of health and sanitation, all for which Western society today is suffering the consequences—not to mention anxieties of an international nuclear war that resulted from human ambition and curiosity that split the atom. Chesterton was right that the Titans have not and will not succeed in ever scaling heaven, but in their efforts, they may destroy the world in the process.[29] Yet, the modern world continues to be excited about every new age and surge of technical and scientific progress—now the digital and robotics frontier—as if these creative marvels hold out only great blessings and not great perils for the human condition. In the words of Reinhold Niebuhr, the "vain delusions" of human imagination as "a gradually evolving god" turned out to be a naïve optimism in human freedom, mastery of nature, and inevitable progress that was refuted by concrete historical realities including two devastating global wars and the creation of atomic weapons: "Every technical advance, which previous generations regarded as a harbinger or guarantor of the redemption of mankind from its various difficulties, has proved to be the cause, or at least the occasion, for a new dimension of ancient perplexities."[30]

Early twentieth-century science fiction novels, such as the works of Asimov, sounded a prophetic warning, imagining the unintended problems of increasing technological dependency and the goal of easing or replacing human labor by robotics.[31] The more intelligent the creations, the more dependent humanity becomes. As humans have no power to predict or control what becomes of the works they create in a spirit of curiosity and desire for greater power and freedom, the more likely it is for autonomous and human-like machines to go rogue literally or metaphorically, defying

---

28. Shelley, *Frankenstein*, 208.

29. Chesterton, *Orthodoxy*, 147.

30. Niebuhr, *Faith and History*, 1, 7, 15, 30, 78, 83. "History does not move forward without catastrophe, happiness is not guaranteed by the multiplication of physical comforts, social harmony is not easily created by more intelligence, and human nature is not as good or as harmless as had been supposed." Niebuhr, "Optimism, Pessimism, and Religious Faith," in Brown, *Essential Reinhold Niebuhr*, 9.

31. Asimov, *I, Robot* and *The Naked Sun*.

the original purpose of the creators: "All normal life . . . consciously or otherwise, resents domination. If the domination is by an inferior, or a supposed inferior, the resentment becomes stronger."[32]

This applies to the history of revolutionary social and political movements as well as technological change. Bonhoeffer observed how the creation of revolutionary liberation from monarchy and aristocracy in France also brought about the "horrible reign of the guillotine" in the new Republic. He even refers to a "basic law of history." The quest for "absolute freedom" paradoxically results in the "deepest servitude." The "master" becomes a "slave," and what is created becomes the "enemy." Liberation "as an absolute ideal" deifies humanity and ultimately leads to the "self-destruction of human beings."[33] Likewise, Chesterton describes how human institutions, even those that began with the noble intent to reform the old, always become old themselves. Ambitions for liberty become new forms of tyranny. The makers of the free capitalist economy of modern industry in the nineteenth century met the "cry of the Socialist that he was a tyrant eating the people like bread."[34] Then, the enforcement of equality brought forth a new form of repression of liberty in Communism. Marx may have been right to criticize failures in the modern industrial-capitalist system of the 1800s, even that many Christians propped up this system rather than sounding a confrontational voice against its excesses, but his utopian conclusions that the end of private property in an atheistic communist state would lead to a more just and perfect society was refuted by historical reality and failed to account for the inescapable reality of sin.[35] In the end, prideful boasting in human freedom and mastery of nature ended up being an illusion—heaven scoffed at the self-righteous efforts of creatures living in an imperfectible world to overcome sin,[36] separated from union with the fullness of God's Spirit and the glories of heaven.

It may seem as if humans have indeed achieved a greater mastery and freedom over nature in making a better world and increasing human fulfillment, but as "the technical mechanism develops which allows us to escape natural necessity," says French philosopher Jacques Ellul, "the more we are

---

32. Asimov, *I, Robot*, 119, 203, 224.
33. Bonhoeffer, "Ethics," 121–24.
34. Chesterton, *Orthodoxy*, 119.
35. Niebuhr, *Faith and History*, 210, 218, 228–29.
36. Niebuhr, *Beyond Tragedy*, 16–17, 18.

subjected to artificial technical necessities."[37] Within the belief that nature can finally be conquered and mankind can be totally free lies a hidden enslavement to the very *means* designed to bring freedom. "Each new power won by man is a power over man as well," states Lewis in *The Abolition of Man*. "Each advance leaves him weaker as well as stronger. . . . Man's conquest of Nature turns out, in the moment of its consummation, to be Nature's conquest of Man."[38]

New solutions of technology and statecraft created new problems, and none of them have successfully resolved the moral problems of humanity: "For twenty centuries the sum total of evil has not diminished in the world. No paradise, whether divine or revolutionary, has been realized."[39] Bonhoeffer speaks of the "illusion" of idolatrous dominion and the false gospel of technology in his work *Creation and Fall* (1959): "The reason we fail to rule, however, is because we do not know the world as God's creation and do not accept the dominion we have as God-given but seize hold of it for ourselves. . . . There is no dominion without serving God; in losing the one humankind necessarily loses the other."[40]

Worldviews defined by a confidence in scientific-technological materialism opened new ways to manipulate human personality under authoritarian structures of technique, propaganda, and efficiency.[41] Alternative forms of tyranny and subjugation were birthed from dreams of personal and national glory. Political criticism of the injustices of liberal capitalism that were answered by the idealistic promises of secular, socialist utopianism exploited modern economic, social, and psychological sciences to create repressive systems of terror, despotic control, and mass dehumanization—as creatively depicted in Soviet-censored Russian and British fictional writings of the early twentieth century.[42]

---

37. Ellul, *Technological Society*, 429; Gay, *Way of the (Modern) World*, 82, 90, 95, 99–100.

38. Lewis, *Abolition of Man*, in *Signature Classics*, 720–21, 724. Our addicted dependency upon iPhones is a case in point.

39. Camus, *Rebel*, 303–4.

40. Bonhoeffer, *Creation and Fall*, 66–67; also, Bonhoeffer, *Ethics*, 115–17; Treier, "Technology Coming of Age," 91–112. Though not a Christian or theist, Camus also affirms, after the blood of revolutionary terror and totalitarianism in the modern age, that "in order to be a man," we must "refuse to be a god." Camus, *Rebel*, 306.

41. Gay, *Way of the (Modern) World*, 210–11, 223–24; Niebuhr, *Faith and History*, 82–83.

42. Figes, *Revolutionary Russia*, 190–203. For more on the relationship of Soviet

Meanwhile, inspired by the writings of Jean-Jacques Rousseau, nineteenth-century German Romantics ushered a new revolt of the spiritual self in rebellion against all constraining social systems, religious *and* rational, ennobling personality-centered intuition, feeling, and the authenticity of the individual.[43] Building from a subjective aesthetic and tied to the quest of self-discovery and fulfillment, what Bellah et al. recognize in American culture as the modern focus on the therapeutic,[44] degeneration into moral license and the breakdown of communal and social bonding was Romanticism's bitter fruit. This could be interpreted as a secular *eros*.

The spirit of modern humanity as it experienced a new consciousness of freedom *over* history and nature to create, in the corruption of its pride, self-love, and a desire to break all bonds restraining creatureliness, also possessed the power of its own self-destruction under the judgment of God:

> Sin is, in short, the consequence of man's inclination to usurp the prerogatives of God, to think more highly of himself than he ought to think, thus making destructive use of his freedom by not observing the limits to which creaturely freedom is bound. Man is at variance with God through this abortive effort to establish himself as his own lord. . . . The Promethean attempt in Eden to snatch wisdom in order to live a life that would (supposedly) be enhanced by being independent of God was a recipe not for human nobility but for human degradation.[45]

This is what David Meyers alludes to as the "American Paradox." Americans are, as a whole, "better paid, better fed, better housed, better educated, and healthier" than in previous centuries, and in comparison to much of the world, having "more human rights, faster communication, and more convenient transportation than we have ever known." Yet at the same time, without a restraining moral referent beyond themselves, postmodern Americans are simultaneously confronted with increasing numbers of suicide, violence, incarceration, divorce rates, fatherless children, and

---

nationalism, industrial progress, and Stalin's Five-Year Plan and to the Ukrainian Holodomor, see Gamache, *Gareth Jones*. For literary criticism of Communism in fiction, see Zamyatin, *We*, and Orwell, *Animal Farm* and *1984*.

43. Rousseau, "Second Discourse"; Wulf, *Magnificent Rebels*.
44. Bellah et al., *Habits of the Heart*, 47–48.
45. Niebuhr, *Faith and History*, 104–5, 109, 121–23, 164, 232–33.

a society virtually on the brink of abandoning all traditional and rational-universal moral values for chaos.[46]

The Same Old Story: Eden and Babel

The perils of modern humanity resemble an ancient problem that stretches back to the opening chapters of the Torah. The fault does not lie exclusively with technology or progress per se. It is the proud ambition and over-confidence of the human spirit that motivates it. Some might be tempted to romanticize the monastic withdrawal of the ancient desert fathers, rural families of Pennsylvania Amish, or the Transcendentalist vision of a return to unspoiled, natural goodness. Yet as Stevenson's *The Strange Case of Dr. Jekyll and Mr. Hyde* depicts, human nature at its core remains a duality. It was the evil side (Hyde) caged and controlled by inward moral constraints and outward social expectations that, once a door to freedom was cracked, raged stronger with the will to be unleashed and overcome Jekyll.[47] William Golding's *Lord of the Flies* strands several British boys on a primitive island left free of modern civilization's constraints to make their own society and rules. The will to survive in the harsh, untamed wilderness, however, devolved into a spiteful competition of clashing egos between Jack and Ralph and a violent thirst for dominance. "Fancy thinking the Beast was something you could hunt and kill!" spoke the pig's head impaled on a stick to the mind and imagination of Simon. "I'm part of you? Close, close, close! I'm the reason why it's no go? Why things are what they are?"[48]

Genesis three is the archetype, or the "mirror" of history. The serpent's temptation to eat of the tree and join him in rivaling God, rendering him unnecessary, was extended through an appeal to covetousness of God's independence and authority as a repression of human potential. As poetically explored by Milton in *Paradise Lost*, the serpent enticed the mother of all the living with doubts of the creator's truthfulness and goodness, that he was jealously protecting his own privilege of freedom, knowledge, and power that was available equally to mankind: "Those rigid threats of Death; ye shall not Die; How should ye? By the fruit? It gives you Life To Knowledge: By the Threat'ner [God]? Look on mee, Mee who have touch'd and

---

46. Myers, *American Paradox*, 5, 138. In the new age of modernity, the "only truth is the Unique." Camus, *Rebel*, 63.

47. Stevenson, *Strange Case of Dr. Jekyll*.

48. Golding, *Lord of the Flies*, 58, 164.

tasted, yet both live, And life more perfect have attain'd than Fate Meant me, by vent'ring higher than my Lot."⁴⁹ Trying to become gods without God, to defy their creatureliness and dependency, humanity's idolatrous freedom is always frustrated by the realities of finitude and death (Eccl 1:18–23). Whether individually or collectively, human beings sin in vainly striving on their own to bring paradise to earth.

The story of Babel in Gen 11 further symbolizes the "pretensions of human cultures and civilizations." It first shows that the human race is oriented toward transcendence and permanence ("He has set eternity in the human heart," Eccl 3:11), possessing a restlessness to push against creaturely limits, but it also characterizes the ambitious goal of ultimate mastery of self and the world without God as doomed from the start.⁵⁰ In defiance of God's will, Babel represents the "desire to exclude God from his creation," of the aspirations and boasts of human collectivity to master the world and to bring human flourishing without God: "They want to name themselves. In fact, they want to make a name for themselves. . . . It means becoming independent, and that is what their attempt at building meant. The people wanted to be definitively separated from God."⁵¹ Contrast God's declaration to make mankind, "Let us make mankind in our image" (Gen 1:26), to the successors of Nimrod at Babel: "Come, let us build ourselves a city" (Gen 11:4). It was not their creativity that God condemned, gifts that were God-given, but their *egoistic* use of those gifts, boastfully in defiance of God, thinking they could overcome the limits of their creatureliness embedded within the historical process to become their own gods over creation. One hears from the mouth of Nebuchadnezzar, the king of Babylon, several centuries later an echo of the same pride that resulted in his own humiliating fall. "Is not this the great Babylon I have built as the royal residence, by my mighty power and for the glory of my majesty?" (Dan 4:30). Concerning the self-confidence of mankind, "God himself has resolved that they shall

---

49. Milton, *Paradise Lost and Regained*, 214 (bk. 9, lines 685–90).

50. "Every civilization and every culture is thus a Tower of Babel." Niebuhr, *Beyond Tragedy*, 27–30. See also 100–101, 161–62, 201, 211–12, 222–23, 246. As with the fall in Gen 3, Niebuhr interprets these as symbolic and emblematic myths of the universal possibilities and problems of prideful human freedom limited by historical finitude. Although he denies that these are actual historical events, his insights into the historical typology of these biblical stories offers a profound critique of modern secular culture. For example, Niebuhr likens Babel to the Empire State Building in New York, a "perfect symbol of pride of a commercial civilization," which was erected at the very same moment in US history as the Great Depression. See 40–41.

51. Ellul, *Meaning of the City*, 15–17.

not succeed.... The road to Paradise, whether viewed as the way back or the way ahead, is now barred to rebel mankind.... No godless heaven will ever be found, or built, on earth, no matter how far we search or how hard we try. God has decreed that utopianism will fail."[52] In the end, however, the power of human ego (self-love) corrupts all human ideals and achievements, dooming them to mortality, and it is God alone who builds the only perfect and enduring city for the humble who in dependence have loved him (Heb 13:14–15).[53]

Collectively, modern society succumbed to the ancient heresy of Pelagianism in believing that it inherently holds the power to fulfill its own ultimate redemption and perfection in history, transmuting rational ideals and potentialities of a perfect world order into historical realities through independent rational knowledge, moral optimism, and more scientific progress. Trying to perfect this world collectively without *dependence* upon God is ultimately a vision of creating a world *without* God—as creaturely dependence is one of the fundamental attributes that defines human identity. Unsurprisingly, call it the judgment of God or the logical consequence of the unnatural misuse of his creation, the historical reality has not panned out to that vision but rather looks more like the futility characterized in the myth of Sisyphus. The dream of the Enlightenment has been shattered by secular nationalism, philosophical nihilism, dehumanizing violence and injustice, and the chaos of moral relativism. "If we wish to pull down the prosperous oppressor we cannot do it with the new doctrine of human perfectibility," Chesterton says, "we can do it with the old doctrine of Original Sin."[54] In other words, it is not in listening to the siren call of Pelagian self-sufficiency, but rather the humbling warnings of Augustinianism. It is human creatureliness, sinfulness, and the admission of personal and collective limitations that—in dependence upon God—drive people to seek him who bestows forgiveness, wisdom, and strength: "It certainly appears paradoxical that exaltation abases and humility exalts," Augustine reflects. "But devout humility makes the mind subject to what is superior.... Exaltation ... spurns subjection for that very reason.... By aiming at more, a man is diminished, when he elects to be self-sufficient and defects from the

---

52. Packer and Howard, *True Humanism*, 24–28; Niebuhr, *Faith and History*, 71, 77–78, 83; Niebuhr, *Beyond Tragedy*, 166.

53. Augustine, *City of God*, 881 (bk. 19, ch. 21); Niebuhr, "Christian Church in a Secular Age" and "Augustine's Political Realism," in Brown, *Essential Reinhold Niebuhr*, 84, 131, 138–40.

54. Chesterton, *Orthodoxy*, 148.

one who is really sufficient for him . . . it is not something that comes from man, but something above man, that makes his life blessed; and this is true not only of man but of every heavenly dominion and power whatsoever."[55]

The boasts of human knowledge and power are alluring, but independent of God continue to cut humans off from the tree of immortal life (Gen 3:22–23). The temptations of throwing off human restraints are the same old deceptions, seducing humanity with the idolatrous promises of knowledge, power, and freedom, but masking a destructive spirit that leads to death. The modern creed of human self-sufficiency is contradicted by the creation-fall-redemption narrative of Scripture and apostolic faith that *is* the reality of human history: mankind's creaturely dependence, fall into corruption, ultimate subjection to decay and death of all creation, and the only hope for complete restoration to glory assured in the mercy of the incarnation, righteousness, and resurrection life of Jesus Christ, the Son of God.[56]

Integration of the Four Loves and Christianity in a Secular Age

Lest the purposes of the above be misunderstood, this is no panegyric for the premodern world of Christendom, which witnessed its own history of wars, cruelties, and injustices. In fact, the fracturing of the Christian love of God to excesses in history (and thereby its corruption) may have played at least some part in the rise of the secular option in the modern age. Integration of these four loves is not to be confused with any wish or program to return worldly power into the hands of Christians, but the preserving of a full and living alternative to the popular modern secular worldview—which at its very root is the unrestrained pride of humanity (an idolatrous desire) to make and have the whole world without God. Much less a grand solution to change the modern Western cultural drift, although perhaps the West might see a return one day to traditional Christian beliefs and practices once the secular project has run its course and failed, loving God

---

55. Augustine, *City of God*, 572–73 (bk. 14, ch. 13), 891–93 (bk. 19, chs. 25–26). In his discussion of the Tower of Babel, Augustine states that the "safe and genuine highway to heaven is constructed by humility." Augustine, *City of God*, 657 (bk. 16, ch. 4).

56. So states the Apostles' Creed: "I believe in God, the Father almighty, creator of heaven and earth. I believe in Jesus Christ, his only son, our Lord, who was conceived by the Holy Spirit and born of the virgin Mary. He suffered under Pontius Pilate, was crucified, died, and was buried; he descended to hell. The third day he rose again from the dead. He ascended to heaven and is seated at the right hand of God the Father almighty."

through the four loves preserves the truthful story about the human condition and challenges the one being sold incessantly by modern humanism with its enticing promises and optimism.

Where organized church religion is seen as increasingly irrelevant in a modern world enamored by its own choices to make the most of life, loving God through participation in the liturgy of worship (*storge*) is to join collectively to humbly offer thanksgiving and publicly acknowledge through the repetition of word and sacramental symbol absolute dependence of individual and social humanity upon the mercy of a transcendent God, immanent in Jesus Christ and the gift of the Holy Spirit. In gathering, churches confess that it is he who will bring the ultimate and permanent psychological, social, economic, and ecological healing for which creation groans. The perfection of the world, the return to Eden, is only realized as humanity is united with the triumph of Christ against all evil, a story which is retold again and again through communal worship and engagement in the formational cycles and structures of sacred liturgy.

Against the selfishness that characterizes the modern pursuit of happiness in the hoarding of private prosperity, the chasing after personal glory, fame, and fulfillment, and the freedom promised by power and wealth, loving God in friendship with Christ (*philia*) is to steward life as he did—sacrificially, generously, and with humility for the well-being, salvation, and honor of others. As essential as evangelism and adherence to classical Christian orthodoxy is, this love also reminds Christians that loving God in a secular age is more than intellectual and verbal quarrels about truth. It is a living apology, a selfless love and sacrifice for others that will not be resisted and cannot be refuted (Prov 25:22). True friendship with Christ also involves union with a risen and living Person, a supernatural power that speaks against the pride and self-sufficient moralism of human reason and will disconnected from the spiritual life and empowerment of God.[57]

Contrary to the pervasive spirit of Romanticism that encourages people to respect their own inner voices, to follow their own desires, dreams, and ideals, discovering their own truth and authentic self within themselves, and idolizing the pleasure and beauty of romantic human love, loving God in desire for union with him (*eros*) expresses a deep human hunger to touch a personal power that is not of—or bound to the processes of—this world, an invisible and infinite life and power transcendent to the self and sensible world and yet in whom "we live and move and have our

---

57. Maritain, *Three Reformers*, 122–23, 128.

being" (Acts 17:28). It is the desire to know and encounter the eternal God who fashioned the human mind, heart, and will from love and in personal union with whom is the satisfying nourishment and energy that feeds created souls in a way that nothing else created can. This union with God has both an intellectual (mind) and affectional (heart) quality. It is both rational and mystical, cognitive and emotional. These have often been pitted against each other in Catholic and Protestant movements of scholasticism and mysticism or pietism. Loving God in *eros* strives to unite the philosophical and theological path of visionary beatitude emphasized in Thomism with the spiritual romance emphasized in Franciscan spirituality and practical imitation of Christ.[58]

Loving God in charity (*agape*) speaks a word against the idol modern secular culture makes of comfort, ease, and prosperity, as well as the lack of any God-given meaning in suffering in Nietzschean nihilism. Unlike *philia*, which *chooses* suffering in the form of self-denial and sacrifice, charity loves God for himself even in pains and sufferings that are *unexplained* and *unchosen*. Even with intellectual theodicy in place, Christians who believe in the sovereignty of God and that suffering is the consequence of living in a fallen world still cannot help but *feel* opposed to pain. Even when there is a temptation to "give vent to anger" in pain and to refuse "to pardon God," who has the power to do something but did not or will not, there "is a fight to go on remaining in the love of God."[59] Loving God in the face of unwilled suffering (*agape*) is more a choice than a feeling, the choice to continue worshiping him in the liturgy of thanksgiving, praise, and surrender (*storge*), to choose to see even in suffering a ministry to serve the vision and quest of the kingdom (*philia*), and to choose to seek the soul's eternal pleasure and satisfaction in sweet desire and personal communion with God (*eros*). This is perhaps the strongest challenge to a secular age that there is a God, and he is our true Beloved.

---

58. Chesterton, *St. Thomas Aquinas*, 32. "Whether the supreme ecstasy is more affectional than intellectual is no very deadly matter of quarrel among men who believe it is both, but do not profess even to imagine the actual experience of either." Chesterton, *St. Thomas Aquinas*, 69.

59. Taylor, *Secular Age*, 306.

Afterword
A Dialogue of the Four Loves

IN THE EARLY EVENING, *the four loves*—Eros, Philia, Storge, *and* Agape—*joined each other for drinks at the pub as they were accustomed to do every Thursday. At one point, their jovial conversation turned to the question who among them was the greatest. Eros,* clutching his pipe and leaning back in his chair, was the first to make his case through a thin veil of smoke and the aroma of fried cod.

EROS: I would say I am the greatest of all loves for I am the strength of desire and passion. I am the force of hunger and thirst. I inhabit desperation. I exist to make the two one, over mountain and treacherous sea. There is no risk too high in me to hinder the desire for union and possession. I fill dreams and occupy thoughts. I bring delight and joy in the depths of being. When I am there, they need naught else but each other. All is consumed in me.

PHILIA: But what else do your lovers share?

EROS: Only me. What else is there?

PHILIA: But is there not more to living than the desire of lovers? What else would there be if lovers just ate and drank of you all day long? It seems that you would be the death of them and ultimately of yourself.

EROS: True, where I exist, nothing else compares or matters. My lovers would rather have me in destitution than to have all health and wealth but be apart. Even death is preferable to loss of me. Can you not see how my strength rivals divinity? No wonder, of all the loves, it is I who am most like a god.

Afterword

PHILIA: But it seems your existence depends on mutual desire. What if one desires but the other does not? To always desire but never possess. What despair! What insatiable hunger! And even if there is mutual desire, what if one lover is lost? How painful must that be to fall from such heights of ecstasy to such depths of sorrow. Yes, I admit you possess great power to lift to heaven but also an equal power to cast down to hell. I foresee potential in you to cause as much anger, hatred, and pain as joy, love, and pleasure.

EROS: Yes, there is always risk. But unrequited desire or absence and loss only enlarges my strength the more. Lovers would rather taste me and suffer in anguish than to never know my soaring transports. Yes, for lovers to be parted from me, this causes agony. But does it not make me all the greater that on account of me they would be willing to risk suffering such pain even for a passing experience of rapture in me?

STORGE: So, your strength and existence and immortality rests on *not* acquiring what is desired? You are *desire* for union and possession, but not union and possession itself? Would you not, like any other natural hunger, then, become extinguished the moment you are fed? It seems that you can only live and thrive when what is desired is never fully possessed. Thus, either what is desired is never possessed or if possessed, you become expired. You have a very short lifespan, do you not?

EROS: This is where you misunderstand me, and I should have explained myself earlier. I am the desire between lovers for union, to have nothing between, to be entangled in each other. All else besides matters not. All else is intrusion and interruption where I seek to bond two together. However, what I did not explain is that I can never be fully fed. For although the two seek as much as possible to be one, and in some measure, lovers do attain a mysterious solidarity, yet they also remain numerically two. There is both union and yet distinction. For that, I will always live because possession will always be out of reach. In other words, I will be partially and temporarily but never fully fed, and even then, as one remembers a sweet dessert, the feeding is but the foundation of further desire.

STORGE: So, it seems you are strongest and most alive in ultimately hindering the very possession and union that is desired.

EROS: Yes, in this is my immortality.

STORGE: Yet if desire is never fully met, it may cause the false deception that you can be satisfied elsewhere, in another lover perhaps. Indeed, what is to keep desire from being for the pleasure of desire itself?

EROS: This is also true. But the casualties I may cause do not negate my power. In fact, I believe they endorse it. The pleasure of desire is the risk of pain. You cannot have the former without the latter.

AGAPE: Let me interject a thought or two. You are born of desire and therefore need, are you not?

EROS: This is true. I am. I cannot exist without these.

AGAPE: Then you are a bond that turns lovers in on themselves to fulfill their own desires and needs. You are ultimately a love of self then? What the lovers really love is not so much each other purely in and of themselves but what they receive in and from that which they love?

EROS: I cannot totally deny this, although I cannot exist without adoration. One does not desire to possess what one does not adore first.

AGAPE: It seems that you consist as the bond between only two. As you said, no one or nothing else compares when you are present. You are not universal then. You are powerful indeed but quite limited in scope.

EROS: That is not my concern.

AGAPE: Then it does not seem that you can be the greatest.

PHILIA: I am glad you have said all this, *AGAPE*, which I believe makes me the greatest of all loves. I am a bond open to more individuals that share a common passion for something beyond themselves. In me, they see the world together in much the same way. They share interests, values, and tastes. They are not turned on each other but they are turned together toward the world, and its pleasures are illumined and expanded the more they are shared.

EROS: But since you are turned outward rather than toward each other, that bond seems weaker than mine. And what really bonds you is not each other but that thing that you share. That is what they love, for without that, you would not even exist.

PHILIA: I concede. But you are defining your greatness by intensity. I am defining my greatness in terms of enlargement. You would be content for

Afterword

lovers to gaze in adoration at each other for all eternity. I reward with a much fuller experience of reality. Whereas you would reduce the universe down to two people, I take two or more people and open the joys of exploring and sharing in the world together.

STORGE: But it seems that you are not as intense as EROS. So, what is there in you that is immortally binding? Interests, values, and tastes can change. EROS can stay strong, even stronger, in separation and absence. You are more apt to dissipate over time with a loss of proximity. What becomes of you then? Also, are you strong enough to hold together when there is some grave offense? And your bond, though perhaps more open, can never be equally shared among more than a handful.

AGAPE: Yes, I agree, for it seems, PHILIA, that you, like EROS, are not universal either. You might enlarge a circle, but to be a friend to some is by nature to exclude others. To share you between a few or several is to set others apart and outside. And even within that circle, there is potential for inequality and jealousy that could rival the intensity of EROS. Thus, it appears you are not the greatest of all loves.

By this point, the four loves had left the pub, and had continued their disputation on a walk through the neighboring cobblestone streets and lamplit public gardens. Storge, *looking up at the bright half-moon above, with one hand pinching a smoldering cigarette and the other laying comfortably in the pocket of his tweed jacket, broke the momentary silence between them.*

STORGE: Now, I have my chance to explain why I am the greatest. We have seen the limits of both EROS and PHILIA. EROS can cause as much pain as pleasure. EROS can also, by nature, never be satisfied as it exists as the desire to possess. PHILIA may open the enjoyment of something in common for a greater number, but it is also weak because in its highest form it is limited to at most four, and it still lacks something to bond it closer together through the passing of time and change. Of all the loves so far, I am the one whose reach is broadest and sustains the longest. The bonds of PHILIA and EROS can be as easily broken as they are easily established. What binds together in me more than anything else is the familiarity that comes with sharing time and space. There may be little else in common, but time and proximity are enough to cause my longer duration.

EROS: It seems, however, that you would be the love that goes most unnoticed, the one with the greatest potential to be taken for granted and ignored, and therefore the weakest in intensity and devotion. An affection of familiarity over time may increase your warmth certainly, but you may also breed scorn or lull to sleep. You may not even really be noticed or appreciated until a loss or separation, after which it would be too late.

PHILIA: I agree. *EROS* is alive in desire for possession, and I live where common interests and values are shared and enjoyed. But you, *STORGE*, barely appear to be alive at all.

STORGE: Yes, but you both fail to understand that where you see weakness, I declare my strength. When you are strongest, your presence is more visible, and for you, *EROS*, attention can even turn to you more than that which is loved. I am strongest when less visible. I do not need to make a show of myself. It is in my nature to exist where there is less awareness of my presence. This may lead to a lack of appreciation as you say, but it can also result in a deeper and unshakable veneration. Comfort and belonging are born of familiarity and enable greater transcendence, making me the most enduring of all the loves.

AGAPE: Yet, like the other loves, though perhaps more than they, you are still not universal for you also are exclusive, which in your case is to that which has shared some familiar time and space. For these reasons, you cannot be the greatest of all loves.

AGAPE: Now I will put forth my argument as to why I am the greatest of all loves. Unlike *EROS*, I exist as the desire only to give, not to possess. It is not necessary that what I love be lovable to me or possess any intrinsic worth or characteristic I desire. In fact, I exist to make what is unloved or unlovable into that which is. As we have heard, also, *EROS* might exist in one where it is not shared between two. *PHILIA* needfully exists between two or more. *EROS* and *STORGE* come closer to me in existing even without mutuality, and *EROS* was right in stating that this resembles the power of divinity. Yet, reciprocity in *EROS* and *PHILIA* is still desired. But it is my nature to be strongest where none is received or even expected. This makes me the greatest of all loves because I sacrifice the most, even more than the passionate boasts of *EROS* or *STORGE*'S loyalty of belonging. Can there be a greater love than that which purely desires the good of another and to give without any regard to itself? Unlike all three of you, I am most universal. There is no exclusion or bounds to my life because there is no desire to possess, no common interests or values to be shared, and no familiarity of

Afterword

belonging. I am purely indiscriminate. It is my very nature to be borderless. Therefore, I am the greatest of all loves because my strength and my existence is without condition, and my reach extends universally without limit.

EROS: Does this mean, then, that you feel no grief or pain of loss since you are all giving without self-regard? Why does that make you the greatest and most sacrificing of all loves? It seems that I would be greater since my existence is not without pain.

AGAPE: Yes, I concede that you are indeed not without a willing sacrifice. I do not deny that. But the pain you cause results from self-regard in the one who loves. I am saying that the greatest love gives without self-regard. It starts with none and gives without any need. It is turned purely outward. In you, *EROS*, such self-regard has been known to lead to contempt and hatred as *PHILIA* has already argued. Murder and suicide are often not without origins in *EROS*. I would also argue that my existence knows pain, but the pain is more about what is suffered in that which is loved.

PHILIA: But if you are universal and indiscriminate in your reach, then you are equally shared by all and there is no measuring of your intensity as with *EROS*, *PHILIA*, or *STORGE*. Where all are equal, there is no more or less. Even the word "great" itself becomes meaningless without measurement.

STORGE: Agreed. *PHILIA* has made a strong point. What is your answer?

AGAPE: Indeed. It seems that you have turned my professed strength on its head. Yes, in my universality, I do not discriminate my generosity toward lovers, friends, or family, and nay, it is my crowning glory to be bestowed upon enemies. That makes me impossible to measure in intensity between them as you have argued, but you fail to appreciate one crucial detail. As each of you are great in your own right and might coexist with each other, lovers who are also friends for example, yet it is my universality alone that can encompass and even add strength to all of you. A rejected or faithless lover, a betrayed friend, and a disregarded parent or child. What love has the power to restore each of you to your former glory? Only me. So, you see, not only do I claim to be the greatest of all loves for I alone am indiscriminate and universal, but my generosity also adds to and sustains your own greatness as well.

Our True Beloved

The four loves reached the end of their walk and parted company graciously, agreeing to ponder the foregoing friendly and spirited conversation until their next meeting the following Thursday at the same place and time.

Bibliography

Allen, John. *Rabble-Rouser for Peace: The Authorized Biography of Desmond Tutu*. New York: Free Press, 2006.
Aquinas, Thomas. *Selected Writings*. Edited by Ralph McInerny. New York: Penguin, 1998.
Aristotle. *The Nicomachean Ethics*. Translated by Harris Rackham. Hertfordshire, UK: Wordsworth Classics of World Literature, 1996.
Armstrong, Chris. *Medieval Wisdom for Modern Christians: Finding Authentic Faith in a Forgotten Age with C. S. Lewis*. Grand Rapids: Brazos, 2016.
Asimov, Isaac. *I, Robot*. New York: Del Rey, 2020.
———. *The Naked Sun*. New York: Bantam, 1991.
Aston, Nigel. *Religion and Revolution in France 1780–1804*. Washington, DC: Catholic University of America, 2000.
Athanasius. *The Life of Antony and the Letter to Marcellinus*. Translated by Robert C. Gregg. Mahwah, NJ: Paulist, 1979.
Augustine. *City of God*. Translated by Henry Bettenson. London, UK: Penguin, 2003.
———. *The Confessions of St. Augustine*. Translated by Rex Warner. New York: A Mentor Book, 1963.
———. *The Trinity*. Translated by Edmund Hill, edited by John E. Rotelle. The Works of Saint Augustine: A Translation for the 21st Century, part 1, vol. 5. 2nd ed. Hyde Park, NY: New City, 2016.
Austin, Victor Lee. *Friendship: The Heart of Being Human*. Grand Rapids: Baker Academic, 2020.
Basil the Great. *On Social Justice*. Translated by C. Paul Schroeder. Crestwood, NY: St. Vladimir's Seminary Press, 2009.
Bauckham, Richard. "'Only the Suffering God Can Help': Divine Impassibility in Modern Theology." *Themelios* 9:3 (April 1984) 6–12.
Beale, G. K., and Mitchell Kim. *God Dwells among Us: A Biblical Theology of the Temple*. Downers Grove, IL: InterVarsity, 2014.
Bebbington, David W. *The Dominance of Evangelicalism: The Age of Spurgeon and Moody*. Downers Grove, IL: InterVarsity, 2005.
Bellah, Robert N., et al. *Habits of the Heart: Individualism and Commitment in American Life, with a New Preface*. Berkeley: University of California Press, 2008.
Benedict. *The Rule of St. Benedict in English*. Edited by Timothy Fry. New York: Vintage Spiritual Classics, 1998.
Bergler, Thomas E. *The Juvenilization of American Christianity*. Grand Rapids: Eerdmans, 2012.

Bibliography

Bernard of Clairvaux. *Selected Works*. Translated by G. R. Evans. New York: Paulist, 1987.

Boethius. *The Consolation of Philosophy*. Translated by V. E. Watts. New York: Penguin, 1969.

Bonhoeffer, Dietrich. *Creation and Fall: A Theological Exposition of Genesis 1–3*. Dietrich Bonhoeffer Works, edited by John W. de Gruchy 3. Translated by Douglas Stephen Bax. Minneapolis: Fortress, 2004.

———. *Ethics*. Dietrich Bonhoeffer Works, edited by Clifford J. Green, 6. Translated by Reinhard Krauss, et al. Minneapolis: Fortress, 2005.

———. *Letters and Papers from Prison*. London: SCM, 1971.

Boyd, Craig A., and Don Thorsen. *Christian Ethics and Moral Philosophy: An Introduction to Issues and Approaches*. Grand Rapids: Baker Academic, 2018.

Bromiley, Geoffrey W., ed. *The International Standard Bible Encyclopedia*. Vol. 3, K–P. Grand Rapids: Eerdmans, 1986.

Brown, Dale W. *Understanding Pietism*. Rev. ed. Nappanee, IN: Evangel, 1996.

Brown, Robert McAfee. *The Essential Reinhold Niebuhr: Selected Essays and Addresses*. New Haven: Yale University Press, 1986.

Bunyan, John. *Pilgrim's Progress*. Abbotsford, WI: Aneko, 2014.

Callisen, Christian Thorsten. "Georg Calixtus, Isaac Casaubon, and the Consensus of Antiquity." *Journal of the History of Ideas* 73:1 (2012) 1–23.

Calvin, John. *Institutes of the Christian Religion*. Vol. 2. Edited by John T. McNeill. Translated by Ford Lewis Battles. Westminster, PA: Westminster, 1960.

Cameron, Euan. *Interpreting Christian History: The Challenge of the Church's Past*. Oxford: Wiley-Blackwell, 2005.

Camus, Albert. *The Rebel: An Essay on Man in Revolt*. Revised and translated by Anthony Bower. New York: Vintage International, 1991.

Casey, Michael. *Sacred Reading: The Ancient Art of Lectio Divina*. Liguori, MO: Liguori/Triumph, 1995.

Chadwick, Owen. *The Secularization of the European Mind in the Nineteenth Century*. New York: Cambridge University Press, 1975.

Chan, Simon. *Liturgical Theology: The Church as Worshiping Community*. Downers Grove, IL: IVP Academic, 2006.

———. *Pentecostal Theology and the Christian Spiritual Tradition*. London, UK: Sheffield Academic, 2003.

Chesterton, G. K. *Orthodoxy*. New York: Image, 2014.

———. *St. Thomas Aquinas and St. Francis of Assisi*. Thirsk, UK: House of Stratus, 2008.

Chrysostom, John. *On Wealth and Poverty*. Translated by Catharine P. Roth. Crestwood, NY: St. Vladimir's Seminary Press, 1981.

Cicero, Marcus Tullius. *How to Be a Friend: An Ancient Guide to True Friendship*. Translated by Philip Freeman. Princeton, NJ: Princeton University Press, 2018.

Cohen, S. Marc, et al., eds. *Readings in Ancient Greek Philosophy: From Thales to Aristotle*. 2nd ed. Indianapolis: Hackett, 2000.

Compendium of the Social Doctrine of the Church. Pontifical Council for Justice and Peace. Washington, DC: Libreria Editrice Vaticana, 2011.

Cowper, William. "God Moves in a Mysterious Way." In *The Methodist Hymnal: Official Hymnal of the Methodist Church*, 215. Nashville: Methodist Publishing House, 1966.

Cox, Harvey. *Fire from Heaven: The Rise of Pentecostal Spirituality and the Reshaping of Religion in the Twenty-First Century*. New York: Addison-Wesley, 1994.

Bibliography

———. *The Secular City: Secularization and Urbanization in Theological Perspective*. New York: Macmillan, 1966.
Dante Alighieri. *The Inferno*. Translated by John Ciardi. New York: Signet Classics, 2009.
———. *The Paradiso*. Translated by John Ciardi. New York: Signet Classics, 2009.
———. *The Purgatorio*. Translated by John Ciardi. New York: Signet Classics, 2009.
Descartes, René. "I Think, Therefore I Am . . ." In *The Portable Enlightenment Reader*, edited by Isaac Kramnick, 181–85. New York: Penguin, 1995.
Dorsett, Lyle. "C. S. Lewis and the Care of Souls." *Sensucht: The C. S. Lewis Journal* 7/8, (2013–2014) 89–100.
———. *Seeking the Secret Place: The Spiritual Formation of C. S. Lewis*. Ada, MI: Brazos, 2004.
Dostoyevsky, Fyodor. *The Brothers Karamazov*. Translated by David McDuff. New York: Penguin, 2003.
———. *Demons*. Translated by Richard Pevear and Larissa Volokhonsky. New York: Vintage Classics, 1994.
———. *The House of the Dead*. Translated by David McDuff. New York: Penguin, 2003.
Douglass, Frederick. *Narrative of the Life of Frederick Douglass, an American Slave*. New York: Barnes & Noble Classics, 2003.
Downing, David C. *Into the Region of Awe: Mysticism in C. S. Lewis*. Downers Grove, IL: InterVarsity, 2005.
Dreher, Rod. *The Benedict Option: A Strategy for Christians in a Post-Christian Nation*. New York: Sentinel, 2018.
Durham, Geoffrey. *The Spirit of the Quakers*. New Haven: Yale University Press, 2010.
Edwards, Jonathan. "Religious Affections." In *A Jonathan Edwards Reader*, edited by John E. Smith, et al., 137–71. New Haven: Yale University Press, 1995.
Eliot, T. S. "From *The Idea of a Christian Society*." In *Selected Prose of T. S. Eliot*, edited by Frank Kermode, 285–91. New York: Harcourt Brace Jovanovich, 1975.
Ellul, Jacques. *The Meaning of the City*. Translated by Dennis Pardee. Grand Rapids: Eerdmans, 1970.
———. *The Technological Society*. Translated by John Wilkinson. New York: Vintage, 1964.
Erasmus. "Praise of Folly." In *The Essential Erasmus*, translated by John P. Dolan, 94–173. New York: Meridian, 1964.
Erb, Peter C., ed. *Pietists: Selected Writings*. New York: Paulist, 1983.
Evans, Christopher H. *The Kingdom Is Always but Coming: A Life of Walter Rauschenbusch*. Grand Rapids: Eerdmans, 2004.
Feuerbach, Ludwig. *The Essence of Christianity*. Translated by George Eliot. Buffalo: Prometheus, 1989.
Figes, Orlando. *Revolutionary Russia, 1891–1991*. New York: Picador, 2014.
Fischer, Louis. *Gandhi: His Life and Message for the World*. New York: Mentor, 1982.
Foster, Richard. *Streams of Living Water: Celebrating the Great Traditions of the Christian Faith*. San Francisco: HarperSanFrancisco, 1998.
Gaddy, C. Welton. *A Love Affair with God: Finding Freedom and Intimacy in Prayer*. Foreword by Henri J. M. Nouwen. Nashville: Broadman & Holman, 1995.
Gamache, Ray. *Gareth Jones: Eyewitness to the Holodomor*. Cardiff: Welsh Academic, 2018.
Gay, Craig M. *The Way of the (Modern) World: Or, Why It's Tempting to Live as If God Doesn't Exist*. Grand Rapids: Eerdmans, 1998.

Bibliography

Glyer, Diana Pavlac. *Bandersnatch: C. S. Lewis, J. R. R. Tolkien, and the Creative Collaboration of the Inklings*. Kent, OH: Black Squirrel, 2016.

Golding, William. *Lord of the Flies*. New York: Penguin, 2017.

González, Justo L., and Catherine Gunsalus González. *Worship in the Early Church*. Louisville: Westminster John Knox, 2022.

Gregory, Brad S. *The Unintended Reformation: How a Religious Revolution Secularized Society*. Cambridge: Belknap Press of Harvard University Press, 2012.

Gross, Bobby. *Living the Christian Year: Time to Inhabit the Story of God*. Downers Grove, IL: InterVarsity, 2009.

Hahn, Scott W., ed. *Catholic Bible Dictionary*. New York: DoubleDay, 2009.

Hansen, Walter. "Augustine and C. S. Lewis on Friendship." *Journal of the Marion E. Wade Center* 35 (2018) 19–30.

Harnack, Adolf. *What Is Christianity?* Translated by Thomas Bailey Saunders. New York: Harper Torchbooks, 1957.

Hendrix, Scott H. *Martin Luther: Visionary Reformer*. New Haven: Yale University Press, 2015.

Henry, Carl. *The Uneasy Conscience of Modern Fundamentalism*. Grand Rapids: Eerdmans, 1947.

Hippolytus. *On the Apostolic Tradition*. 2nd ed. English version with introduction and commentary by Alistair C. Stewart. Yonkers, NY: St. Vladimir's Seminary Press, 2015.

d'Holbach, Baron. "No Need of Theology . . . Only of Reason . . ." In *The Portable Enlightenment Reader*, edited by Isaac Kramnick, 140–49. New York: Penguin, 1995.

Ireton, Kimberlee Conway. *The Circle of the Seasons: Meeting God in the Church Year*. Downers Grove, IL: InterVarsity, 2008.

Jaegher, Paul de, ed. *An Anthology of Christian Mysticism: The Basic Writings of the Greatest Christian Mystics*. Translated by Donald Attwater et. al. Springfield, IL: Templegate, 1977.

Jägerstätter, Franz. *Letters and Writings from Prison*. Edited by Erna Putz. Translated by Robert A. Krieg. Maryknoll, NY: Orbis, 2009.

Janz, Denis R. *World Christianity and Marxism*. New York: Oxford University Press, 1998.

Jenkins, Philip. *The New Faces of Christianity: Believing the Bible in the Global South*. Oxford: Oxford University Press, 2006.

———. *The Next Christendom: The Coming of Global Christianity*. Oxford: Oxford University Press, 2002.

Jenson, Robin. "Baptismal Rites and Architecture." In *Late Ancient Christianity*, edited by Virginia Burrus, 117–44. A People's History of Christianity 3. Minneapolis: Fortress, 2005.

Johnson, Maxwell E. "The Apostolic Tradition." In *The Oxford History of Christian Worship*, edited by Geoffrey Wainwright and Karen B. Westerfield Tucker, 32–76. Oxford: Oxford University Press, 2006.

———. "Worship in Late Antiquity." In *Historical Foundations of Worship: Catholic, Orthodox, and Protestant Perspectives*, edited by Melanie C. Ross and Mark A. Lamport, 62–84. Grand Rapids: Baker Academic, 2022.

Justin Martyr. "The First Apology of Justin, the Martyr." Edited and Translated by Edward Rochie Hardy. In *Early Christian Fathers*, edited and translated by Cyril C. Richardson, 242–89. New York: Touchstone, 1996.

Bibliography

Kant, Immanuel. "An Answer to the Question: What Is Enlightenment? (1784)." In *Perpetual Peace and Other Essays on Politics, History, and Morals*, translated by Ted Humphrey, 41–48. Indianapolis: Hackett, 1983.

Kater, Michael H. *Hitler Youth*. Cambridge: Cambridge University Press, 2004.

Kidd, Thomas S. *America's Religious History*. Grand Rapids: Zondervan Academic, 2019.

Kierkegaard, Søren. *Fear and Trembling: Dialectical Lyric by Johannes de Silentio*. Translated by Alastair Hannay. New York: Penguin, 1985.

King, Martin Luther, Jr. "Letter from a Birmingham Jail." In *The Autobiography of Martin Luther King, Jr*, edited by Clayborne Carson, 187–204. New York: Warner, 1998.

Klayman, Seth N. "Messianic Jewish Worship and Prayer." In *Introduction to Messianic Judaism: Its Ecclesial Context and Biblical Foundations*, edited by David Randolph and Joel Willitts, 51–60. Grand Rapids: Zondervan, 2013.

Larsen, Timothy. *Friends of Religious Equality: Nonconformist Politics in Mid-Victorian England*. Studies in Modern British Religious History. Suffolk, UK: Boydell and Brewer, 1999.

Leiva-Merikakis, Erasmo. *Love's Sacred Order: The Four Loves Revisited*. San Francisco: Ignatius, 2000.

Lem, Stanislaw. *His Master's Voice*. Translated by Michael Kandel. Cambridge: MIT Press, 2020.

———. *The Invincible*. Translated by Bill Johnston. Cambridge: MIT Press, 2020.

———. *Solaris*. Translated by Joanna Kilmartin and Steve Cox. San Diego: Harvest Book, 1970.

Lepojärvi, Jason. "Praeparatio Evangelica—or Deaemonica? C. S. Lewis and Anders Nygren on Spiritual Longing." *Harvard Theological Review* 109:2 (2016) 207–32.

Lewis, A. J. *Zinzendorf the Ecumenical Pioneer: A Study in the Moravian Contribution to Christian Mission and Unity*. Bethlehem, PA: Moravian Church in America, 1962.

Lewis, C. S. *The Collected Letters of C. S. Lewis*. Edited by Walter Hooper. 3 vols. San Francisco: HarperOne, 2009.

———. *The C. S. Lewis Signature Classics*. San Francisco: HarperOne, 2017.

———. *The Four Loves*. San Diego: Harcourt, 1960.

———. *God in the Dock: Essays on Theology and Ethics*. Edited by Walter Hooper. Grand Rapids: Eerdmans, 1970.

———. *The Last Battle*. San Francisco: HarperCollins, 2001.

———. *Letters of C. S. Lewis*. Edited by W. H. Lewis and Walter Hooper. San Francisco: HarperOne, 1988.

———. *Letters to Malcolm: Chiefly on Prayer*. New York: Harcourt, 1992.

———. *Perelandra: A Novel*. New York: Scribner, 2003.

———. *The Pilgrim's Regress*. Wade annotated ed. Edited by David C. Downing. Grand Rapids: Eerdmans, 2020.

———. *The Problem of Pain*. New York: Macmillan, 1947.

———. *The Silver Chair*. New York: Harper Trophy, 2000.

———. *That Hideous Strength*. New York: Scribner, 2003.

———. *The Weight of Glory and Other Addresses*. New York: Macmillan, 1949.

Lindberg, Carter. *Beyond Charity: Reformation Initiatives for the Poor*. Minneapolis: Fortress, 1993.

Litfin, Brian. *Getting to Know the Church Fathers: An Evangelical Introduction*. Grand Rapids: Brazos, 2007.

Bibliography

Lubac, Henri de. *The Motherhood of the Church*. Translated by Sr. Sergia Englund, OCD. San Francisco: Ignatius, 1971.

Luther, Martin. "Fraternal Agreement on the Common Chest of the Entire Assembly at Leisnig." Translated by Walther I. Brandt. In *The Christian in Society II*, edited by Walther I. Brandt, 176–94. Luther's Works 45. Philadelphia: Fortress, 1962.

———. *The Freedom of a Christian, 1520*. Annotated Luther Study ed. Edited by Tim Wengert. Minneapolis: Fortress, 2016.

———. "Obedience of a Common Chest, Preface, 1523." Translated by Albert T. W. Steinhaeuser and Walther I. Brandt. In *The Christian in Society II*, edited by Walther I. Brandt, 159–75. Luther's Works 45. Philadelphia: Fortress, 1962.

———. "On Trade and Usury, 1524." Translated by Charles M. Jacobs and Walther I. Brandt. In *The Christian in Society II*, edited by Walther I. Brandt, 231–310. Luther's Works 45. Philadelphia: Fortress, 1962.

Lynn, Monty L. *Christian Compassion: A Charitable History*. Eugene, OR: Wipf & Stock, 2021.

MacHaffie, Barbara J. *Her Story: Women in Christian Tradition*. Philadelphia: Fortress, 1986.

Machen, J. Gresham. *Christianity and Liberalism*. New ed. Grand Rapids: Eerdmans, 2009.

MacSwain, Robert, and Michael Ward, eds. *The Cambridge Companion to C. S. Lewis*. Cambridge: Cambridge University Press, 2010.

Madame Guyon. "Spiritual Torrents (Late 1600s)." In *In Her Words: Women's Writings in the History of Christian Thought*, edited by Amy Oden, 245–49. Nashville: Abingdon, 1994.

Mannermaa, Tuomo, and Kirsi I. Stjerna. *Christ Present in Faith: Luther's View of Justification*. Minneapolis: Fortress, 2005.

Maritain, Jacques. *Three Reformers: Luther, Descartes, Rousseau*. Providence: Cluny, 2020.

Marlowe, Christopher. *Doctor Faustus*. Edited by David Wootton. Indianapolis: Hackett, 2005.

McGrath, Alister. *Christian History: An Introduction*. Chichester, UK: Wiley-Blackwell, 2013.

———. *Christianity's Dangerous Idea: The Protestant Revolution—A History of Christianity from the Sixteenth Century to the Twenty-First*. San Francisco: HarperOne, 2008.

McLeod, Hugh. *Religion and the People of Western Europe 1789–1989*. New ed. Oxford: Oxford University Press, 1997.

———. *Secularization in Western Europe, 1848–1914*. New York: St. Martin's Press, 2000.

Meeks, Wayne A. "The Grammar of Christian Practice." In *The Origins of Christian Morality: The First Two Centuries*. New Haven: Yale University Press, 1993.

Middleton, J. Richard. *A New Heaven and a New Earth: Reclaiming Biblical Eschatology*. Grand Rapids: Baker Academic, 2014.

Milavec, Aaron. *The Didache: Text, Translation, Analysis, and Commentary*. Collegeville, MN: Liturgical, 2003.

Milton, John. *Paradise Lost and Regained*. Edited by Christopher Ricks. New York: Signet Classics, 2010.

Moltmann, Jürgen. *The Crucified God: The Cross of Christ as the Foundation and Criticism of Christian Theology*. Translated by R. A. Wilson and John Bowden. New York: Harper & Row, 1974.

More, Thomas. "Utopia." In *Three Early Modern Utopias*, edited by Susan Bruce, 3–148. Oxford: Oxford University Press, 2008.

Bibliography

Myers, David G. *The American Paradox: Spiritual Hunger in an Age of Plenty*. New Haven: Yale University Press, 2000.
Niebuhr, H. Richard. *Christ and Culture*. New York: Harper Torchbooks, 1956.
Niebuhr, Reinhold. *Beyond Tragedy: Essays on the Christian Interpretation of History*. New York: Charles Scribner's Sons, 1937.
———. *Faith and History: A Comparison of Christian and Modern Views of History*. New York: Scribner, 1937.
———. *Moral Man and Immoral Society: A Study in Ethics and Politics*. Louisville: Westminster John Knox, 2013.
Noll, Mark. *The Civil War as a Theological Crisis*. Chapel Hill: University of North Carolina Press, 2006.
———. *God and Race in American Politics: A Short History*. Princeton: Princeton University Press, 2008.
Noll, Mark, et al. *Turning Points: Decisive Moments in the History of Christianity*. 4th ed. Grand Rapids: Baker Academic, 2022.
Nouwen, Henri. *The Way of the Heart: The Spirituality of the Desert Fathers and Mothers*. San Francisco: HarperOne, 1981.
Nussbaum, Martha C. *Upheavals of Thought: The Intelligence of Emotions*. Cambridge: Cambridge University Press, 2001.
Nygren, Anders. *Agape and Eros*. Philadelphia: Westminster, 1953.
Okholm, Dennis. *Monk Habits for Everyday People: Benedictine Spirituality for Protestants*. Grand Rapids: Brazos, 2007.
Olson, Roger. *The Mosaic of Christian Belief: Twenty Centuries of Unity and Diversity*. Downers Grove, IL: InterVarsity, 2002.
Orwell, George. *1984*. New York: Signet, 1961.
———. *Animal Farm*. New York: Signet Classics, 2020.
Ozment, Steven. *The Age of Reform, 1250–1550*. New Haven: Yale University Press, 1980.
Packer, J. I., and Thomas Howard. *Christianity: The True Humanism*. Waco, TX: Word, 1985.
Pak, G. Sujin. "Scripture, the Priesthood of All Believers, and Applications of 1 Corinthians 14." In *The People's Book: The Reformation and the Bible*, edited by Jennifer Powell McNutt and David Lauber, 33–51. Downers Grove, IL: InterVarsity, 2017.
Parratt, John, ed. *An Introduction to Third World Theologies*. Cambridge: Cambridge University Press, 2004.
Pascal, Blaise. *Pensées*. Translated by Alban J. Krailsheimer. New York: Penguin, 1966.
Payton, James R., Jr. *Light from the Christian East: An Introduction to the Orthodox Tradition*. Downers Grove, IL: IVP Academic, 2007.
Perl, Carl Johann, and Alan Kriegsman. "Augustine and Music: On the Occasion of the 1600th Anniversary of the Saint." *Musical Quarterly* 41:4 (1955) 496–510.
Peterson, Michael L. *C. S. Lewis and the Christian Worldview*. Oxford: Oxford University Press, 2020.
Phillips, Edward L. "Worship in the Early Church." In *Historical Foundations of Worship: Catholic, Orthodox, and Protestant Perspectives*, edited by Melanie C. Ross and Mark A. Lamport, 47–61. Grand Rapids: Baker Academic, 2022.
Pico della Mirandola, Giovanni. *Oration on the Dignity of Man*. Translated by A. Robert Caponigri. Washington, DC: Regnery, 1956.
Piper, John. *Desiring God: Meditations of a Christian Hedonist*. Rev. ed. Portland, OR: Multnomah, 2011.

Bibliography

———. *Let the Nations Be Glad: The Supremacy of God in Missions*. 30th anniversary ed. Grand Rapids: Baker Academic, 2022.

Postman, Neil. *Technopoly: The Surrender of Culture to Technology*. New York: Vintage, 1993.

Pseudo-Dionysius. "The Mystical Theology." In *Pseudo-Dionysius: The Complete Works*, 133–42. Translated by Colm Luibheid. New York: Paulist, 1987.

Raboteau, Albert J. *Canaan Land: A Religious History of African Americans*. Oxford: Oxford University Press, 2001.

Rana, Fazale R., with Kenneth R. Samples. *Humans 2.0: Scientific, Philosophical, and Theological Perspectives on Transhumanism*. Covina, CA: Reasons to Believe, 2019.

Rauschenbusch, Walter. *Christianity and the Social Crisis in the 21st Century: The Classic That Woke Up the Church*. San Francisco: HarperOne, 2007.

Reeves, Michael. *Delighting in the Trinity: An Introduction to the Christian Faith*. Downers Grove, IL: InterVarsity, 2012.

Rempel, John D. *Recapturing an Enchanted World: Ritual and Sacrament in the Free Church Tradition*. Downers Grove, IL: InterVarsity, 2020.

Richardson, Cyril C., ed. *Early Christian Fathers*. New York: Touchstone, 1996.

Roberts, Alistair. "Liturgical Piety." In *Our Secular Age: Ten Years of Reading and Applying Charles Taylor*, 63–74. Deerfield, IL: The Gospel Coalition, 2017.

Roberts, J. Deotis. *Black Religion, Black Theology: The Collected Essays of J. Deotis Roberts*. Edited by David Emmanuel Goatley. Harrisburg, PA: Trinity Press International, 2003.

Robinson, John A. T. *Honest to God*. 40th anniversary ed. Louisville: Westminster John Knox, 2002.

Rolle, Richard. *The Fire of Love*. Translated by Clifton Volters. London: Penguin, 1972.

Romero, Oscar. *The Violence of Love*. Translated by James R. Brockman. Maryknoll, NY: Orbis, 2004.

Rose, June. *Elizabeth Fry: A Biography*. London: Papermac, 1981.

Rosell, Garth M. "Foreword." In *William Wilberforce, A Practical View of Christianity*, edited by Kevin Charles Belmonte, ix–xii. Peabody, MA: Hendrickson, 1996.

Ross, Melanie C. "Evangelical Practices of Worship." In *Historical Foundations of Worship: Catholic, Orthodox, and Protestant Perspectives*, edited by Melanie C. Ross and Mark A. Lamport, 253–66. Grand Rapids: Baker Academic, 2022.

Ross, Melanie C., and Mark A. Lamport, eds. *Historical Foundations of Worship: Catholic, Orthodox, and Protestant Perspectives*. Grand Rapids: Baker Academic, 2022.

Rousseau, Jean-Jacques. "The Second Discourse: Discourse on the Origin and Foundations of Inequality among Mankind." In *The Social Contract and the First and Second Discourses*, edited by Susan Dunn, 69–148. New Haven: Yale University Press, 2002.

———. "The Social Contract." In *The Social Contract and the First and Second Discourses*, edited by Susan Dunn, 149–256. New Haven: Yale University Press, 2002.

Rudolph, David. "Messianic Judaism in Antiquity and in the Modern Era." In *Introduction to Messianic Judaism: Its Ecclesial Context and Biblical Foundations*, edited by David Randolph and Joel Willitts, 21–36. Grand Rapids: Zondervan, 2013.

Russell, Jeffrey Burton. *Prince of Darkness: Radical Evil and the Power of Good in History*. Ithaca, NY: Cornell University Press, 1988.

Ruth, Lester, and Lim Swee Hong. *A History of Contemporary Praise and Worship: Understanding the Ideas That Reshaped the Protestant Church*. Grand Rapids: Baker Academic, 2021.

Bibliography

Schmemann, Alexander. *For the Life of the World.* Yonkers, NY: Saint Vladimir's Seminary Press, 2018.

Scriven, Joseph M. "What a Friend We Have in Jesus." In *The Methodist Hymnal: Official Hymnal of the Methodist Church,* 261. Nashville: Methodist Publishing House, 1966.

Shakespeare, William. *The Tragedy of Romeo and Juliet.* In *The Riverside Shakespeare,* edited by G. Blakemore Evans, 1055–99. Boston: Houghton Mifflin, 1974.

Shelley, Mary. *Frankenstein.* New York: Barnes & Noble Classics, 2003.

Smith, James K. A. *Imagining the Kingdom: How Worship Works.* Grand Rapids: Baker Academic, 2013.

———. *You Are What You Love: The Spiritual Power of Habit.* Grand Rapids: Brazos, 2016.

Smith, Timothy L. *Revivalism and Social Reform: American Protestantism on the Eve of Civil War.* Baltimore: Johns Hopkins University Press, 1980.

Sobrino, Jon. *Archbishop Romero: Memories and Reflections.* Rev. ed. Translated by Robert R. Barr, et al. Maryknoll, NY: Orbis, 2016.

Spener, Philip Jacob. *Pia Desideria.* Translated by Theodore G. Tappert. Minneapolis: Fortress, 1964.

Spink, Kathryn. *Mother Theresa: An Authorized Biography.* Revised and updated. San Francisco: HarperOne, 2011.

Steffan, Truman Guy, ed. *Lord Byron's Cain: Twelve Essays and a Text with Variants and Annotations.* Austin: University of Texas Press, 1968.

Stevenson, Robert Louis. *The Strange Case of Dr. Jekyll and Mr. Hyde, and Other Stories.* Edited by George Stade. New York: Barnes & Noble Classics.

Strauss, David Friedrich. *The Life of Jesus, Critically Examined.* Translated by George Eliot. 3 vols. Cambridge: Cambridge University Press, 2010.

Straw, Carole. *Gregory the Great: Perfection in Imperfection.* Berkeley: University of California Press, 1991.

Sunquist, Scott W. *The Unexpected Christian Century: The Reversal and Transformation of Global Christianity, 1900–2000.* Grand Rapids: Baker Academic, 2015.

Sweeney, Douglas. *The American Evangelical Story: A History of the Movement.* Grand Rapids: Baker Academic, 2005.

Synan, Vinson. *The Holiness-Pentecostal Tradition: Charismatic Movements in the Twentieth Century.* 2nd ed. Grand Rapids: Eerdmans, 1997.

Taylor, Charles. *A Secular Age.* Cambridge: Belknap Press of Harvard University Press, 2007.

———. *Sources of the Self: The Making of Modern Identity.* Cambridge: Harvard University Press, 1989.

Tel, Martin. "Calvinist and Reformed Practices of Worship." In *Historical Foundations of Worship: Catholic, Orthodox, and Protestant Perspectives,* edited by Melanie C. Ross and Mark A. Lamport, 178–91. Grand Rapids: Baker Academic, 2022.

"The Temple of Reason." In *The Portable Enlightenment Reader,* edited by Issac Kramnick, 168–73. New York: Penguin, 1995.

Teresa of Avila. *The Interior Castle.* Translated by Mirabai Starr. New York: Riverhead, 2003.

Thomas à Kempis. *The Imitation of Christ.* Translated by Ronald Knox and Michael Oatley. Providence: Cluny Media, 2023.

Thurman, Howard. *Jesus and the Disinherited.* Boston: Beacon, 1996.

Bibliography

Tiffany, Grace. "C. S. Lewis: The Anti-Platonic Platonist." *Christianity and Literature* 63:3 (Spring 2014) 357–71.
Tocqueville, Alexis de. *Democracy in America*. English ed. Vol. 1. Edited by Eduardo Nolla. Translated by James T. Schleifer. Carmel, IN: Liberty Fund, 2012.
Tolstoy, Leo. "Religion and Morality." In *A Confession and Other Religious Writings*, translated by Jane Kentish, 129–50. New York: Penguin, 1987.
———. "What Is Religion and of What Does Its Essence Consist." In *A Confession and Other Religious Writings*, translated by Jane Kentish, 81–128. New York: Penguin, 1987.
Tomkins, Stephen. *William Wilberforce: A Biography*. Grand Rapids: Eerdmans, 2007.
Treier, Daniel J. "Technology Coming of Age in Bonhoeffer's Apocalyptic Proverbs." In *Bonhoeffer, Christ, and Culture*, edited by Keith L. Johnson and Timothy Larsen, 91–112. Downers Grove, IL: InterVarsity, 2013.
Trueman, Carl R. *The Rise and Triumph of the Modern Self: Cultural Amnesia, Expressive Individualism, and the Road to Sexual Revolution*. Wheaton, IL: Crossway, 2020.
Tutu, Desmond. *No Future Without Forgiveness*. New York: Image, 1999.
Vainio, Olli-Pekka. "The Aporia of Arguments from 'Love': A Meditation on C. S. Lewis' Four Loves." *Chronicle of the Oxford University C. S. Lewis Society* 4:2 (May 2007) 21–30.
Volf, Miroslav. *After Our Likeness: The Church as the Image of the Trinity*. Grand Rapids: Eerdmans, 1997.
Voltaire. *Candide*. London: Arcturus, 2018.
Wainwright, Geoffrey, and Karen B. Westerfield Tucker, eds. *The Oxford History of Christian Worship*. Oxford: Oxford University Press, 2006.
Walls, Andrew. *The Missionary Movement in Christian History: Studies in the Transmission of Faith*. Maryknoll, NY: Orbis, 1996.
Walsh, James, and P. G. Walsh. *Divine Providence and Human Suffering*. Message of the Fathers of the Church 17. Wilmington, DE: Michael Glazier, 1985.
Ward, Mary Augusta. *Robert Elsmere*. Edited by Miriam Elizabeth Burstein. Brighton, UK: Victorian Secrets, 2018.
Ware, Timothy. *The Orthodox Church*. New ed. New York: Penguin, 1997.
Warren, Tish Harrison. *Liturgy of the Ordinary: Sacred Practices in Everyday Life*. Downers Grove, IL: InterVarsity, 2016.
Watson, Thomas. *All Things for Good*. Carlisle, PA: Banner of Truth Trust, 1986.
Webber, Robert, and Lester Ruth. *Evangelicals on the Canterbury Trail*. Rev. ed. Harrisburg, PA: Morehouse, 2013.
Wells, H. G. *The Food of the Gods*. In *H. G. Wells: Six Novels*, 493–639. San Diego: Canterbury Classics, 2012.
White, James F. *A Brief History of Christian Worship*. Nashville: Abingdon, 1993.
———. *Protestant Worship: Traditions in Transition*. Louisville: Westminster John Knox, 1989.
Wilken, Robert Louis. *The Spirit of Early Christian Thought: Seeking the Face of God*. New Haven: Yale University Press, 2003.
Williams, George H., ed. *Spiritual and Anabaptist Writers: Documents Illustrative of the Radical Reformation*. Philadelphia: Westminster, 1957.
Williams, Reggie. "Dietrich Bonhoeffer: The Harlem Renaissance and the Black Christ." In *Bonhoeffer, Christ, and Culture*, edited by Keith L. Johnson and Timothy Larsen, 59–72. Downers Grove, IL: IVP Academic, 2013.

Bibliography

Wilson, Derek. "Past Tense and Future Conditional." In *Charlemagne: A Biography*, 189–204. New York: Vintage, 2007.

Wolffe, John. *The Expansion of Evangelicalism: The Age of Wilberforce, More, Chalmers, and Finney*. Downers Grove, IL: InterVarsity, 2007.

Wright, N. T. *Simply Christian: Why Christianity Makes Sense*. San Francisco: HarperOne, 2006.

Wulf, Andrea. *Magnificent Rebels: The First Romantics and the Invention of the Modern Self*. New York: Alfred A. Knopf, 2022.

Young, Sarah. *Jesus Calling*. Nashville: Thomas Nelson, 2004.

Zamyatin, Yevgeny. *We*. Translated by Clarence Brown. New York: Penguin, 1993.

www.ingramcontent.com/pod-product-compliance
Lightning Source LLC
Chambersburg PA
CBHW072153160426
43197CB00012B/2371